Love Letters from Mother Earth

The Promise of a New Beginning

Anneloes Smitsman

Foreword by Alexander Laszlo

Love Letters from Mother Earth

Anneloes Smitsman

Love Letters from Mother Earth - The Promise of a New Beginning

Published by EARTHwise Publications
Quatre Bornes, Mauritius
info@earthwisecentre.org

Paintings © 2017 by Rachel Tribble

Design of cover page and book layout by John Cooper
Pictures of author by Sita Kelly Photography
Original design of figures by Anneloes Smitsman and formatted by John Cooper

First Edition, First in the Series

Printed in the United States of America
First Printing, 2019
ISBN-13: 9781724165466
EARTHwise Publications
Quatre Bornes, Mauritius

*Dedicated to the Eternal Child
in Each of Us*

Acknowledgements

I would like to start by thanking and acknowledging Mother Earth and our Sun for bringing me forth and entrusting me with these ancient wisdom teachings via these thirteen *Letters of Love* (referred to throughout as *Letters*).

There are so many people who I like to thank and acknowledge for all their amazing support and love for me, and for their support with these beautiful *Letters*. First of all, my beloved parents, Ad and Coby Smitsman, for all their incredible Love and unconditional support through my whole life. My dear partner Kurt Barnes for his depth of wisdom and support. He is in many ways a co-author of these *Letters* in our lived understanding of all that is shared here, even though he chose not be named explicitly in that way.

My children, Manu and Akash, for being the inspiration for this book. It is for them and all the children of our world that I wake up each day determined to support the co-creation of a world and future where all of us can flourish and thrive together.

Alexander Laszlo, for writing the foreword for this book with so much elegance and insight, and for his continuous support for me, and this book.

Justine Page for her unwavering support and belief in me and the importance of these *Letters*, and for walking this journey with me in the true spirit of sisterhood. My other sisters who have held space with me during the initial birthing period in 2016: Zenobia Beckett Ryken, Amanda Caza, and Kimberley Montgomery.

Kim Conrad for her masterful editing, and dedication through many hours of deep listening and intuiting with me and Mother Earth for the right choice and sequence of words to share the essence of this wisdom, in a way that makes it accessible to people.

Rachel Tribble, for contributing her amazing art to this book. Her paintings naturally tell the story of these *Letters*, even though her paintings were made before she had read these *Letters*. My dear friend John Cooper, for his beautiful design with the covers of this book and the internal layout.

Colin Davis for proofreading the first draft of the book, and Liba Markson for her wonderful proofreading and editing of the previous edition of these *Letters*.

Joel Bakst for our many hours of meaningful conversations and sharing the teachings of the oral and written codes of the Kabbalah.

My wonderful community of friends and colleagues who have supported me and these *Letters*: Stephane Leblanc, Nicola Hoffman, Jean Houston, Phil Lane Jr, Christopher Chase, Ingrid Frints, Jude Currivan, Shelley Ostroff, Erik Lawrence, Julie Krull, John Greenhalgh, Adam Molyneux-Berry, Daniel Wahl, Anne-Marie LaMonde, Thomas Smith, Melissa Mari, Carolyn Flower, Lawrence Bloom, and many more. For those of you whose names I have not mentioned here, just know you are in my heart, and I thank you all too.

Finally, I would like to thank you, dear reader, for meeting here in this brief moment in time and space, where our thoughts and love connect through these *Letters* as we remember we are all part of the same Family.

Whatever brought you to this book, or in whatever way this book came to you, I trust the timing is just right. It is the nature of wisdom to share. It is in the receiving that the giving is completed. All that has been shared here is with the intention that this may support us to flourish and grow into the beautiful wisdom that we each are. To become, as my dear friend Jean Houston said, *the possible human for a possible world* - a world that is Home for all of us and is Life's deepest *Promise* to each and every one of us. Thank you for being.

Reviews

"Anneloes Smitsman is the leading edge in the studies of consciousness and reality. Her profound explorations in self evolution, quantum physics and social change are both thrilling and unique. I highly recommend this book full of inspiration and wisdom. It provides essential guidance to remember our way home, and becoming the *possible human for a possible world.*"

Jean Houston (Ph.D.)
Chancellor, Meridian University
Author of over 30 books in human development and social change

"Whether you've come to this planet to make a difference, or whether you're lost and confused on how and why you got here, this book is a must read. Anneloes Smitsman explores in depth the core reasons for how our dysfunctional and separated society arose. So this is no lightweight tome. The 3 keys to our salvation are explained in some detail, as well as the reason for our enslavement. She writes: "*Love cannot be divided and fragmented. Knowing this, these false systems attempted to diminish the power of Love by fragmenting and dividing us.*" Thus this enslavement arises from our shared hallucination of the "polarity" matrix, which is the lens through which we see the world, and which blinds us to the unity that lies behind the duality. And so we believe, unwittingly and unconsciously, that we live in a dualistic reality system, seemingly unable to access that Oneness from which all this reality arises. Anneloes shows us a way through this delusion. And now we have reached an extreme point of bifurcation. The book explains that we are at the end of a major series of 16 cycles and it's "crunch time." If you want to know how to be prepared for this unique moment, and you should ...read this book, it will change your life!"

Lawrence Bloom (Ph.D.)
Secretary General, Be Earth Foundation & Chair, Dakia Institute

"*Love Letters from Mother Earth* is a tender, wise and wholehearted gift. Thanks to Anneloes Smitsman's compassionate sensitivity and poetic soul, we are inspired and empowered to hear the voice of our beloved Mother. Love Letters invites us in profound and yet gentle ways to re-member and heal our vital relationship with our one and only planetary home. In re-minding and re-hearting us of not only our reliance on Her but Her ever-loving nurturing of all Her children, it is a vibrant and timely message to help guide our way home."

Jude Currivan (Ph.D.)
Cosmologist, Healer, and Author of *The Cosmic Hologram*

"*Love Letters from Mother Earth*, by Beloved Sister Anneloes Smitsman, is one of those must read books! This book reconnects us to the Sacred Teachings and Beauty of our Beloved Mother Earth in a most beautiful, inspiring, wise, insightful and uplifting way!"

Hereditary Chief Phil Lane Jr.
Ihanktowan Dakota and Chickasaw Nations
Founder & CEO, Four Worlds International Institute

"Anneloes Smitsman has written a singular and unifying document. Or perhaps she has channeled this work. I can't imagine how she did it! Not unlike my favorite music and poetry, this writing has deep intellect, spirituality, and sensuality. This is not a common fairytale. Ms. Smitsman requires the reader to rise up and pay attention to every word. She is deeply exploring levels of human existence and growth. This is a guidebook for sentient beings. A book we've hoped and wished might appear. It is conscious of the human condition. Breathing in, we attend to the depth of all that has come before us. Breathing out, we are prepared for what meets us today."

Erik Lawrence
Saxophonist, Flutist, Composer, Journalist, Poet, Sound Healer
Steering Committee Member, Louis Armstrong Center for Music

"*Love Letters from Mother Earth* is an intimate and empathic *inter-consciousness communication* that gifts the reader with a multi-faceted portal into the vast meta-consciousness of Mother Earth and the "*Heart of Light*" our Sun, and their relationship with each other and with humans within the historic context of the larger evolutionary process. In this loving and challenging invitation to stretch beyond the limits of our current narratives are embedded sacred codes for our collective activation and healing. As the evolved feminine consciousness awakens on the planet, Mother Earth speaks through Anneloes Smitsman with clarity and compassion, wisdom and sensuality to support us in remembering who we are and in shifting beyond a consciousness of hierarchy and polarity to one of greater wholeness. The book reminds us of the need to move beyond our sense of separateness and superiority on the planet, so that we can communicate in deeply honoring ways with consciousnesses beyond our own, and in so doing contribute to our collective healing and evolution. Empathy with Mother Earth and Her experience alongside our own, is indeed an essential starting point for moving beyond our limited pictures of ourselves, healing the trauma and devastation and reconnecting with the Source of all Life. Messaging the archetypal feminine in its primal form, the book, with each re-reading, will undoubtedly shapeshift to reveal new and fertile layers of insight and embodied wisdom."

Shelley Ostroff (Ph.D.)
Founder, Together In Creation

"This book embodies the ethos of wholeness with deep, mystical wisdom complemented by strong, cognitive intelligence. Both come into balance in this book, reminding us how to allow our heart to lead and guide. *Love Letters from Mother Earth* is a rare and precious gift. It is like a luminous wisdom map for every reader to discover his or her own inherent brilliance and step into essential wholeness."

Julie Krull (Ph.D.)
Founding Steward, GOOD of the WHOLE, Talk Radio Host

"Albert Einstein famously reminded us that we will not solve the crises confronting us if we approach them in the same way of thinking that created them in the first place. He called the separation between self and world an 'optical illusion of our consciousness'. *Love Letters from Mother Earth* should be read with this in mind and heart. Anneloes Smitsman writes from the understanding that we all are in fact expressions of a living Earth and hence able to speak not for her but as her. These Letters offer a wealth of insights and expanded perspectives on love, trust, overcoming the illusion of separation, and restoring our internal wholeness. We are invited on "*a journey into our evolutionary potential and unfolding.*" This book is an invitation to re-envision yourself as participant in and co-creative agent of the whole that brought you forth. This participatory way of seeing and relating will help us respond to the converging crises with wisdom. Doing so, we may discover that these crises harbour within them an opportunity of transforming the human impact on Earth by transforming our understanding of who we truly are."

Daniel Christian Wahl (Ph.D.)
Author of *Designing Regenerative Cultures*

"This amazing book is in the same genre as Eckhart Tolle's *The New Earth*, which was published more than 10 years ago. Now, *Love Letters from Mother Earth* takes us a step further and deeper into our understanding of our Planet as a conscious loving being. It is an essential book for our changing world. Anneloes Smitsman, has an incredible access to wisdom and a beautiful way with words that explain why we are in our current paradigm, and how we can help heal our world by re-membering its wholeness, guided by the feminine wisdom of our Mother. This book has the power to awaken our true wisdom potentials, and is a guide to be referred to and read over and over again."

Justine Page
Transformational Coach, Trainer & Public Speaker

"If you want to experience coming alive, more integrated, more connected, more whole than ever before, read this book! If you care about our planet and the future of our children and all of life, read this book. It will enhance your capabilities of making a difference far beyond what words can explain. This book helps you become what you've always wanted from the deepest cells of your being.... Read On and...Welcome Home."

Dame Kim Conrad
Award-winning Author, International Speaker, Executive Coach
Founder of Sacred Life Living, LLC

"Anneloes Smitsman has written a beautiful invocation to find joy on earth. Imbued with love, hope, and faith, the writing is full of compassion as it honours Nature and all its precious beings on earth, in particular men and women (and all gender in between). It is an inspiring text that gives one a sense of being in the world and also beyond the world simultaneously as it delves into the realms of the real, the metaphoric, the poetic, and the mystical. It gives one a sense of becoming one with the Earth and beyond. As I have always been enchanted with the notion of the Akashic records wherein exists four interconnected states of knowing and being called, Holographic Unity, Harmonic Memory, Synchronic Order and the Imaginal Realm, I was immediately drawn to Smitsman's capacity to bring these existential realms to conscious and unconscious knowing through her *Letters*. As each *Letter* brings forth a particular consciousness, it invites us to delve deeply into their meaning to receive a full understanding of our existence as being whole, unified, harmonic, synchronic and, yes, imaginal. The words of Elie Wiesel jump out at me for we must look to meaning and purpose. Yet, what cannot be drawn from a darkness that lies outside our ability to describe, define, or understand it, we must seek instead for a way to say, "*Here there is a why.*" To be cut off from seeking our purpose and raison d'être is a travesty. It is for this reason we can and must seek why as we continue to venture into deeper understandings of love. To come to know the fullness of love takes living life fully and pausing at each step to reflect on its depth and vastness. Each step of the way requires a constant opening, for any shutting down leaves us gasping for air. These *Letters* from Mother Earth present us with yet another opening for inquiry and introspection."

Anne-Marie LaMonde (Ph.D)
Adjunct Professor, University of British Columbia, Canada

"Part prayer, part meditation, part medium transmitted message, part invocation, part direct transmission, part guidebook, part diary of love letters in the tradition of Rumi writing to and of his beloved – *Love Letters* is a reminder of our essential oneness with all that emerges together with us in this dance of life, love, consciousness and light...This is the alchemy needed to transmute the present stage of human being to the next level of our evolutionary potential. This is indeed a book for times to come."

From the foreword by **Alexander Laszlo (Ph.D.)**

"If you enjoyed Rumi or Neale Donald Walsch, you will love this book. It is a message to us all about how we can navigate in this world and restore our deepest connections. With each Letter you will find your own consciousness expanding. I found this a guidebook, a loving reminder of our essential oneness and sacred feminine wisdom. As I read through each chapter I found my own consciousness opening up, evolving, and returning home to the essentials."

Zenobia Beckett
Corporate Leader

"In reading *Love Letters from Mother Earth*, I regained hope for humanity's fate as this beautiful book is full of profound wisdom teachings that allow us to reconnect with our true essence, and gives us the energy to continue on our path of transforming humanity so that we can co-create a promising future for the next generations."

Stéphane Leblanc
Founder & CEO, International Center for Conscious Leadership

Contents

Foreword

$\mathcal{O}$ ver thirty years ago, in their ground-breaking book *Order Out of Chaos*, Nobel Laureate Ilya Prigogine and his co-author Isabelle Stengers observed that "*we are living in a dangerous and uncertain world that inspires no blind confidence.*" Many still subscribe to this view, though more and more we are starting to realize that we are part of a living world and that an underlying *anima mundi* binds the patterns of being and becoming into a coherent narrative of cosmic emergence. And yet... the experience of day-to-day living often seems to be precisely that: dangerous and uncertain. There appears to be no pattern to it, or if there is one, some would affirm that it appears to follow Murphy's Law, according to which "*Anything that can go wrong will go wrong.*" There seems to be no guidance, no one who can provide clear, comforting, or even stern messages by which to navigate Life on Earth. Indeed, when we find ourselves in times of trouble, where is our Wise Mother, our *Alma Mater*, who comes to us, speaking words of wisdom? Let us see...

Over the years and since an early age, Anneloes Smitsman has had many opportunities to absorb words of wisdom - from various peoples and places. She has lived in and been exposed to a variety of cultures, ecosystems, wisdom traditions, ways of knowing, of doing, of being and of experiencing the world within and around us. Forged of Aboriginal Dreamtime and Northern Lights, of Polynesian Wayfaring and the Medicine Wheels of manifold shamanic wisdom traditions, Smitsman's vision penetrates the mysteries that surround and condition human existence. Indeed, it would be hard to say just where - or even when - she is from. And strangely enough, it is precisely this lack of identity that gives her the greatest ability to identify with that which is shared among us all - our home in the cosmos, Planet Earth.

Through this book, Smitsman takes on the role of a medium - a messenger to humanity. *Love Letters from Mother Earth* is a fabulous story, a fable to re-story the narrative of humankind by re-membering our place in the dance of being and becoming with all of the rest of life, it's living processes and of Earth, herself. These "*thirteen letters to find your way home again*" are written in the voice of Mother Earth and comprise an allegory of spiritual communion at a time when the zeitgeist of humanity is steeped in images of despair, devastation, apocalypse, cataclysm, catastrophe and collapse. The entertainment industry churns out one dark saga after another, seemingly celebrating end-times. Amidst this clamor of fatalism and nihilism comes this beautiful book of *Love Letters*, giving hope, a sense of peace, and the means through which to generate our own power to transmute all these energies into light, love and life. Transmuting these energies is important for us to learn, as Mother Earth lets us know: "*Until we manifest the archetypes that are truly wisdom based from the Eternal, this pattern will keep repeating.*"

This is no work of fiction. What Smitsman has done here is much more than to speak for Earth in a fanciful projection of personal predilection. She speaks not with the voice of a human being seeking to represent Earth but rather of one who is an integral part of Earth speaking for herself. These messages, these love letters, anthropomorphize and anthropopathize the planet on which, in which, and through which all of us were born. And they tell us a much needed story - not a bedtime story for little children, but a coming-of-age story for those whose self-identity is changing as we reach a new stage of collective consciousness. Through immersing ourselves in the stories told by the *Love Letters* we don't fall asleep at all. Indeed, the energies and insights that come through this story are keys to a deeper awakening. Smitsman provides a meditation message, a mantra of nature's nurture that comes from, creates, and is best received as a trance-state of flow-being.

Not only does Smitsman share messages that are indeed *Love Letters from Mother Earth* to us, the Children of Earth - her children, she also writes in the voice of our beautiful Sun above and beyond who shares a larger view and a greater context of our cosmic emergence. Furthermore, she writes in the voice of the deepest Consciousness that undergirds all of the manifest universe, that perennial frame of being that remains out of spacetime's reach. The message that comes through on all these levels, from Mother Earth to our beautiful Sun to deepest Consciousness, is that of our essential oneness. Indeed, these levels of narrative are eventually understood as expressions of our own Self, for in the end, *Love Letters from Mother Earth* is a story of unity consciousness.

Part prayer, part meditation, part medium transmitted message, part invocation, part direct transmission, part guidebook, part diary of love letters in the tradition of Rumi writing to and of his beloved - *Love Letters* is a reminder of our essential oneness with all that emerges together with us in this dance of life, love, consciousness and light. This is not the static Oneness of final peace as a resting place of spirit. Not in the least! The oneness of which Smitsman writes, in the voice of Mother Earth, is oneness in motion. This is the flow state of deep harmonization with the life-affirming, future-creating, and consciousness-connecting pattern of evolutionary emergence that flows around and through us.

Too often we turn against this flow and seek fleeting satisfaction - ego satisfaction - in short-term gains that give us a false sense of achievement. These byways and eddies in the greater flow of cosmic becoming seem as traps that make of life little more than a testament to Murphy's Law. Mother Earth helps us gain perspective on this apparent need of ours, this penchant for quick fixes and superficial satisfactions. She points out that: "*The paradox of Life is that we experience the changeless in a world of change; we experience Darkness by contrast of Light, and so forth. We live in a world of duality, yet underlying this is unity. That is what our triunity is all about.*"

She shows us that there are ways out of these traps and offers us keys to our freedom that will unlock the portals of flowing balance and guide us to our ever emerging home in harmony with Earth - our home both within and around ourselves. This home is no fixed place but a flow space of being, a dynamic grace-state of unity - oneness in motion. Mother Earth tells of how: "*For any who are still trapped in this dream of division, may you realize that nobody can keep you asleep. We have everything inside us to awaken and remember our unity."*

Such messages offered in *Love Letters* provide keys to the secrets for unlocking our consonant potential, our connected harmony, and our coherent life force as integral parts of Earth, herself. In short, these are the keys to integral, evolutionary harmony, both within ourselves and with our living Mother Earth.

As you read the messages from Mother Earth, lingering upon the love with which they are written and soaking in the light with which they are infused, you begin to see how they comprise an invitation to join the Dance of Life. And yet, they are so much more than a call to get up and force yourself to dance: they are an invitation to let go and allow yourself to be danced! The difference between trying to dance and letting yourself be danced may seem trivial, but quite literally it makes a world of difference. Mother Earth lets us know that it's okay to let go and allow ourselves to be flowed: "*I embrace you deeply. Don't try to figure it all out with your mind. Trust, and let your wisdom guide you through this. I am with you.*"

According to the worldview currently emerging in the sciences, we live in a holographic and highly integral and interdependent world. The new narrative re-casts the story of cosmic emergence from *The Big Bang* to what Jude Currivan has called *The Big Breath*. The world depicted in this view is like a dance of Universe and Cosmos – with the universe comprising the entirety of manifest being (all phenomena we experience and know through our five senses), and the cosmos comprising a deeper and even broader reality (the noumena that undergird and give rise to the universe). We can't access the cosmos through our five senses alone, but we can know it as an expression of primordial consciousness beyond space and time. Metaphorically, this is the dance of Heaven and Earth. Human beings on Earth are another expression of this dance, like flowers in a garden.

If you consider what's most important for a garden to flourish, would it be the seeds or the greenhouse? Clearly, without the seeds (which represent humans - the systemic leverage points for creative synergy), the creative impulse of the garden is thwarted and its growth and full potential aren't realized. However, without the greenhouse (which represents Earth - the requisite systemic nurturance space), there is no home in which we can grow and our potential cannot be realized. To curate the dynamics of thrivability beyond mere sustainability, it is necessary to create opportunities for seeds to grow and roots to connect such that new visions may emerge and flourishing interdependencies arise.

A new codex is needed, and fortunately, this is precisely and explicitly what Mother Earth provides through the writing of Smitsman. The *Love Letters* serve as state attractors that provide individual inspiration for collective aspiration, showering light, water, air and fertile soil in delicious combinations and quantities for the garden of our individual and collective human being to come into full flourishing. The constant dance between doing and being - between creating conditions for the flourishing of human and all life and getting out of the way so that they can thrive authentically - this is the same dance of Universe and Cosmos, expressed on a different scale. And just as the dynamics of the quantum world are at a different scale than the dynamics of our experiential world, they operate according to different parameters and produce different patterns. But the music of the dance is the same.

With the keys to freedom and a new codex of oneness in motion, *Love Letters* provide much needed guidance and nurturance for navigating life in these times of turbulence and transition. Science is coming to understand that the brain is neither a generator of memories nor a storage space for them but rather a highly specialized organ that serves as a transceiver of information - a type of send/receive antenna that reads-in messages from the underlying cosmic memory field and reads-out messages that align the flows of emergence in our world... or don't (if we misuse or abuse our message transmitting abilities). This memory field has been known in certain spiritual traditions as the Akashic Record and in quantum mechanics as the Zero Point Energy Field. Smitsman is adept at tuning into and accessing this field, though it is an ability that all beings have and one that each of us can learn to use.

Love Letters gives guidance as to how to cultivate this ability.

By learning to use the power of this highly specialized organ, the essential message that comes through is that we are whole beings whose integral existence is what truly transforms the world. In other words, while our brains may be transceivers of information, our whole beings (brain, body, mind and spirit) are transducers of information - transforming and transmuting through-flows of information into coherent patterns of being in relation to our surroundings (both internal as well as external to each of us). Mother Earth urges us to, "*restore the connections with the unified field of consciousness.*"

Clearly, the more we can learn the use of "*Self as instrument*" to tap into this underlying consciousness that informs the patterns of evolutionary emergence, and the more we can align those patterns in ways that increase the coherence, connection and consonance of our presence with Earth and all the life and life support systems of Earth, the more we can then actualize oneness in motion and move into the laminar flow-space of thriving cosmic emergence. How best can we learn to be the Earth at the same time as we manifest cosmic consciousness, and at the same time as we are true to our own human nature?

Mother Earth knows how, and through these *Love Letters*, you will gain a glimpse of how to safeguard and nurture your truest and highest potential as part of the grand narrative of cosmic emergence while avoiding the pitfalls of the more disconnected and egoic expressions of that potential. As she says: "*Your greatest protection from this manipulation, internally and externally, is by staying closely tuned to our innate wisdom, and by connecting with each other from a place of Love. As I shared previously, our direct connection with the unified field of consciousness is the real foundation for our autonomy within the One. It is through this that the Universal becomes localized as you, me, and us. When you see from this awareness, deception becomes visible through the thought-forms and intentions that aim to distort these wisdom qualities and our unity.*"

In *The Wheel of Time* (Carlos Castaneda's work of spiritual guidance gleaned from the teachings of the wisdom tradition in which he was immersed), messages were given for connecting to and working with the cycle of time defining our contemporary era. In *Love Letters from Mother Earth*, Anneloes Smitsman shares messages in the form of spiritual guidance from Mother Earth, herself. These messages are also messages of time. They stand to shift our contemporary zeitgeist from darkness and despair to love and light. This is the alchemy needed to transmute the present stage of human being to the next level of our evolutionary potential. This is indeed a book for times to come.

Alexander Laszlo (Ph.D.)
President, Bertalanffy Center for the Study of Systems Science
Director of Research, Laszlo Institute of New Paradigm Research

Preface

We are living in a time of increasing uncertainties and challenges. Many changes are taking place that are deeply affecting us that have consequences for many generations yet to come. It is precisely in those times of uncertainty and collapse, that the living wisdom and Love from our Planetary Mother is more important than ever.

In 2015, before these *Letters* came into being, I received the following message from Mother Earth: *Remember my Promise*. At that time in 2015, I did not yet realize the depth of Her message. In the years that followed Her message unfolded as a germinating seed. I realize now that these *Letters* are *Her Promise* to us through which she shares with us the wisdom, guidance, and Love to support us through these challenging times.

She is standing by us with all Her Love and strength, as our Mother. Within *Her Promise* is *the Promise* that times will get better after they may first seem to get worse, and that we will find our way Home to each other. Our indigenous wisdom keepers from around the world have shared through their prophecies that this is the time of the great convergence, and the birth of a new cycle of time also called the fifth world. A new evolutionary cycle born from wholeness and unity - *A New Beginning!*

This *Promise* of our Planetary Mother is now in your hands in the form of these thirteen *Letters*. These contain Her wisdom, insights and reminders, together with the wisdom of our Sun, for how we can actualize this cycle of unity promised long ago. This is *the Promise* that we will rise together united in our love, wisdom, and consciousness to bring forth a world and future where all can thrive and flourish together. A new Global Civilization.

The first *Letter* was born in 2016, in the aftermath of the terrorist attacks in Paris when I asked Mother Earth: *As our Planetary Mother what can you share with us, as your children, so we may remember who we are and find our way home to each other during these challenging times?* By listening carefully and letting go of my ideas about these questions, a deeper intuitive knowing emerged. As I started to record what I felt guided to share, it became clear to me that each *Letter* is like a code that helps us see and remember what is already deep within us. These *Letters* form a living map that activates a very deep ancient knowing for how to restore our wholeness and actualize our true humanity.

The cascading effects of our divisions and disunity have escalated into a dangerous ecological tipping point. As we have now entered the time of what is called escalating climate-change and biodiversity loss, we are faced with the possibility of our own extinction. Never before has it been more important to realize that the nature of Life is unified. We are all in this process together. As my dear friend Chief Phil Lane always says, *the hurt of one is the hurt of all, the honor of one is the honor of all.*

The Promise of a New Beginning lives within each of us as an ancient seed code from the Eternal. We have been aware of this possibility for a long time, yet as a species we were not yet sufficiently engaged with the process for birthing this collectively. This is the process of what my dear friend Jean Houston calls *the possible human for a possible world.*

Collective engagement in the birthing of this new possibility is increasing now. Many of us are experiencing the contractions of our collective birthing for this new cycle. It seems we are now entering through the narrow part of our collective birth canal. It is within this context that these *Letters* from Mother Earth and Father Sun have come into being. They remind us that we are made for this process and we are not alone. This is also echoed in the incredible work of thousands of people, organizations, and movements from around the world who stand for the regeneration, healing, and flourishing of our world and planet.

The first thirteen *Letters* form the foundation, as they set the stage for how to birth and become *the possible human for a possible world;* a world where of all of us can flourish and thrive together.

Through the next series, more guidance is provided with greater details about this possibility for our new civilization.

Writing and birthing these *Letters* is a deeply meditative process for me. Each *Letter* comes with particular life experiences that prepare me to bring these messages forth. Each message shared is lived first. I do not take any ownership for these *Letters*; these are not my *Letters*. They flow from our collective wisdom as a gift of guidance, Love, and support. It may take several times of re-reading to receive the depth of the wisdom that is contained within these *Letters*.

After the initial *Letters* were published in 2017, hundreds of people shared with me how this book changed their life by awakening this deep innate knowing that they had forgotten they knew. This updated version is shared from a new platform that better supports these *Letters* to be spread to the four corners of our world. The content of the 13 original *Letters* has also expanded to provide further clarification on key concepts for which it is now the time to share this.

Love Letters from Mother Earth has become a series. This book is the first in this series. You may notice that the words Love, Light, Mother, Father, Self, Life, and Eternal are capitalized. This is out of respect for the concepts they refer to, namely the Eternal changeless reality of our Oneness. The same could be applied to other words as well, yet these specific words have been selected to help us connect with their meaning as Eternal qualities. Furthermore, some words are written in *italics* for emphasis and as a reference to their earlier appearance in a particular context.

To make these teachings more accessible there will soon be a companion guidebook with practices and audio recordings to take you deeper for greater benefit and value from these *Letters*. You can also join my regular online classes where we go deeper together into the application and wisdoms of each *Letter*. All that is shared here is what we live as a community through the EARTHwise Centre. *The Promise of a New Beginning* is what inspires us to live and share this commitment. To join us for any or all of the opportunities above please connect with us. You find our details at the last page.

Thank you for reading these *Letters*. Take all the time you may need for receiving what is shared here. It is recommended to read the book at least once from beginning to end since there is a sequence to the way the sacred principles and *three keys* are shared. For inspiration and intuitive guidance you can also open the book wherever you feel guided to read, and you may discover new meaning in the words again and again. Enjoy also the blank pages of wisdom without words at the end of each *Letter,* they are there for a purpose...

This book is written intuitively to connect with our inner wisdom, and to remember that every one of us is an expression of Mother Earth. It is also written to remind us that the *living book* of Life lives within each of us. As such we are all co-creators of *our* unfolding story, and carry the seed potentials for this *New Beginning*.

It is my deep conviction that together, by actualizing our unity, we can bring forth a whole new world and future where all of us can thrive and flourish. I meet you there.

With gratitude and love,

Anneloes Smitsman
Mauritius, 3 November 2018

Message from Mother Earth

Welcome. I am known by many names: some call me Mother Earth, or Mother Nature, others call me Gaia, Chaya, or Pachamama. Thank you for reading my *Love Letters*. This is not just a book. It is so much more than that...

These *Letters* are an invitation to join me into the heart of our togetherness, to remember an ancient *Promise* that was shared long ago. Through our journey I will share with you the sacred knowledge of *three keys* for actualizing our unity. These keys are already within our wisdom nature, yet unrealized by many. By applying these keys you will come to understand the cause for the divisions in our world, and how we can become the birth for a *new* world and future born from our wholeness and unity, by the power of Love.

Take your time to be with all that is shared here. Some of the information and concepts may require digestion, reflection, and re-reading. It is written in a language that many people are not familiar with, and most are not used to hear my voice in this way. For some this language may feel like finally coming Home. Every word here is shared with the deepest love.

May our journey Home heal our pain, and the roots of our pain. It is time now to re-member deeply who we are, and what was *Promised* long ago. It is time for this wisdom to be shared now in its completeness.

If anything is not clear for you, know that you can always close your eyes and listen with me from your heart. If some of my words or concepts trigger you, please know that this too is ok. All is welcome here, all is blessed.

A *New Beginning* awaits us, let us enter into that together now. Thank you for coming. I love you.

Part 1
Our Beginning

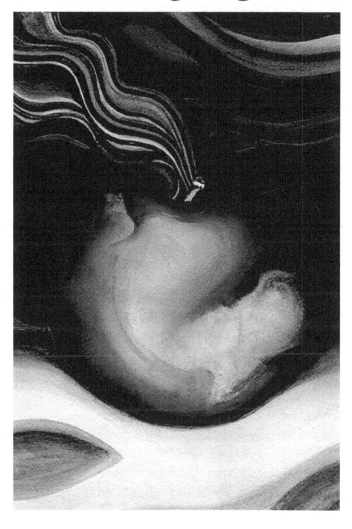

Letter 1
The Flame of Love

Billions of years ago, by the count of the human calendar, my body came into being through a symphony of Love and sacred impregnation through seven rays of Light. In the spectrum of creation, this is not long ago. We are deeply united, as you are each a living cell within my planetary being. Through my forests, rivers, and oceans, I am your breath of Life each day and night. I am also like a guardian and a Mother for the evolution of Life that unfolds through my planetary being. From my womb, impregnated with the sacred Life potentials, I brought you forth into this Life as the human being you now are. My life-giving power of nature lives deep inside each of us. By this power, we can renew and recreate from the sacred seed potentials of the Eternal.

We are living in challenging times, as we are moving in transition between different cycles. My *Letters of Love* are here to provide support for this transition time by reminding you of an ancient *Promise of a New Beginning*. Our first *Beginning* was not able to bring forth the actualization of all our qualities from the Eternal. As we come to realize the deeper why, we also awaken to the keys inside us for actualizing *the Promise* of the living reality of who we truly are. There may be some concepts in my *Letters* that are slightly different from what you have grown accustomed to. I invite you to listen for what is transmitted behind these words, trusting that all will become clear towards the end.

A *New Beginning* becomes possible when humanity realizes that we are the possibility for this world that has long been prophesized by the ancient wisdom keepers. We are each gifted with the seed codes from the Eternal for a world and future born from wholeness and unity, by the power of Love. Yet few have known how to access the keys for activating these seed codes. Once activated, the actualizing of our unity becomes *unstoppable*.

These seed codes are the inner architecture of Life from the Eternal. They serve a specific purpose for our full actualization. When we work with these sacred codes, we will come to understand the Source of our creative power, and how to apply this for the flourishing of ALL Life. These codes are already within you as your true humanity. Honor also the seed codes of the plants, trees, and animals, and their evolutionary potential, before it is too late.

As we learn to work together on restoring our balance, and by healing the many divisions among and within us, these seed codes become activated. As I mentioned earlier, these codes are from the Eternal and are not created by anyone or anything. You, as a human being, were formed from this wisdom. Only the human mind started to turn away from this. This wisdom knows who you truly are and what your purpose is within the larger family of Life.

In part two of my *Letters* you will learn about *the three keys* for accessing these sacred codes and actualizing our unity. You will also learn how to apply these keys for birthing our *New Beginning*. The process toward that is not always easy. I'd like to remind you, therefore, that we are all on this journey together. Each of us matters.

Our journey with you as my human children started long ago. There are some aspects of this journey and our *first* Beginning that I would like to share with you now, to provide a deeper understanding of the challenges we are facing today.

.

An Ancient Story

Long ago a dream emerged from within the One; from this arose the flame of Love. This flame started expanding, and as it expanded so did our universe. This flame needed a sacred place of Love within which it could be received. The flame needed to be received for the One to be known to Itself. As it expanded, seeking the boundaries through which the One could become known to Itself, the counter force to expansion started to emerge from within. Out of this process, gravity manifested.

Through the manifestation of gravity the alchemy of Love, as the sacred flame, was able to become localized through time and space. It was then that my body started to form and I became one of the holders and recipients for the alchemy of Love. Receiving the sacred flame of Love impregnated my being. Within me, as I became a Mother for this world of Life, a great ecstasy of indescribable joy and gratitude arose from the center of my being.

With tears of joy, the deepest Love spread from within me to all the life potentials that now lay pregnant in my womb, for our birth. As my tears of joy and gratitude were overflowing to all that was now within me to bring forth, my oceans and rivers formed. As the flame of Love fertilized my waters, Life started to sprout and evolve.

The process of Life was set in motion, and has continued ever since. This same sacred flame of Love that impregnated my being formed our souls to bring forth all of Love's potentials. From the One, God and Goddess manifested to bring forth the Spirit of Life, which activated the power of creation that is within each of us.

The consciousness that was born from the original Dreaming was not yet mature, not yet stable. There were not yet sufficient bodies and mature relationships to receive, hold, and make manifest this flame of Love in its whole wisdom. The flame of Love was barely Self-aware, it had only just been received by me, and others like me. The relationships were not yet ready to safely guide the maturation process of the consciousness born from this process. The desire of Life to create, and bring Itself forth, expanded and formed this universe that we are in now.

As Life started to evolve from this process, many started to forget our original unity. Time emerged as matter formed, which created an experience of distance between the original Dreaming and our experience of now. This created an experience of memory, whereby the original Dreaming was perceived as the past, rather than a continuous and Eternal reality of the ever-present. In these

4

mental gaps of space-time pockets, a vacuum appeared that gave rise to the formation of intentions to control the flame of Love, and the process of creation.

Beings started to take control of this mental vacuum by desiring to be the God of all. They took the fire of the flame of Love that was within them, and directed this away from the sacred principles for creating from wholeness. Without the application of all the sacred principles guiding creation, the flame of Love could not be made manifest from the wholeness of our deepest union. As such, the potentials it offered only partially manifested. This misuse of creation gave rise to perceptions of duality that became polarized over time. The inner potentiality of our true nature was not yet able to be realized.

Instead the belief in duality and division started to grow and slowly formed a collective mental matrix onto which the experiences of dualistic polarization became further imprinted. This started to influence the unfolding of our collective consciousness fields. Our evolutionary potentials became more and more constrained by these archetypical relationships that were based on the inappropriate use of duality and the polarity principle.

As I will explain more later, the true purpose of polarity is not to divide and separate Life. Polarity within our toroidal movement serves to enable the convergence and fusion of our sacred seed potentials to bring forth a deeper evolutionary bonding. Yet as the true nature of this mental vacuum was not realized, neither was the appropriate use of the polarity principle.

Our unity was not able to actualize in the weaving of the human realms. Partiality instead of wholeness, and division instead of convergence became dominant in humanity's cultures. People's connection with me and Life became more and more distorted via these fractured archetypes. Many forgot our direct Source connection and primordial unity. The original Dreaming was only remembered and kept alive by a small group of my children. The sacred creation principles that maintain the integrity of our unity and wholeness were replaced by the systems that favored the fractured archetypes.

This polarization and dualism also manifested as the belief in heaven and hell. Manipulation and control dynamics gained in force, as it became more challenging to realize our underlying unity. The power of Love, however, could not be manipulated since it represents our primordial unity from the Eternal. Love does not distort reality. Love cannot be divided and fragmented. Knowing this, these false systems attempted to diminish the power of Love by fragmenting and dividing us instead. Suffering increased and more of my children became trapped in these collective blankets of pain and forgetfulness.

The Four Worlds

As the unity of the One came into being, Life started to expand, diversify and evolve. Within this unity are various principles, each playing their sacred role for the full actualization of our divinity into form. Let me share with you briefly here what these sacred principles are about and which processes they guide.

The creative action from the One unfolds as a tri-unity; three as One. In this triunity we also find the principle of two, the duality principle. In the triunity these dual forces are united in their common Source to bring forth a new unity as One, not divide. The triunity, also called the trinity principle, is the alchemical principle of creation. Each new One has within it all the principles for our full actualization, which is explained later in *the Wholeness Code* in *Letter* 3. Each new One is whole.

The manifestation of the creative forces via the triunity principle gave rise to the principle of four. Whereas three gives the dynamism and alchemy required for creation, four gives stability and foundation. This is also called the quadrant structure. This manifestation of the One through the quadrant principle gave rise to the creation of four worlds.

These worlds are stages of how our unity actualizes through an evolutionary process of diversification and *in-formation*. As such these worlds are not dimensions, yet multiple dimensions exist within each of these worlds. When the duality principle became dominant and controlling, the human realms became more polarized. Without the triunity acting within the quadrants, the convergence between these four worlds cannot occur. Our unity was not able to actualize through that time when duality dominated over the other sacred principles. Instead of seeing unity, many people saw the four quadrants through a dualistic lens without recognizing the underlying wholeness.

For convergence to take place within and between the quadrants, which is necessary for evolution to move to its next stage of development, the principle of five is required. This is also the principle of the quintessence. When the four can converge and unite in a common center also seen as the fifth, our unity actualizes and becomes embodied. Through the fifth, the quintessence, all the evolutionary potentials within the quadrants converge and unite to bring forth a new creation.

The fifth then emerges as a new One that embodies the actualization of the integrated, syntonized, and converged evolutionary potentials of the quadrants and the four worlds. This is also described as the fifth world, the birth of a new civilization, a new era, and a new cycle of time. I understand that for some these concepts may be new, and could even be confusing. This process will all become clearer for you when you continue to read the rest of *my Letters*. For now, join me to go back to our *earlier Beginning*.

Long ago by not recognizing and honoring Life as a unified reality, the human realms became more and more divided. This division is also present for many people in their diminished brain coherence. The human brain is also organized in four quadrants. These are known as the left and right brain hemispheres and the lower and higher brain. These four quadrants of the brain are not fully coherent and synergized for many people yet, especially if duality dominates their perception. When there are mental divisions, the quadrants in the brain cannot converge to bring forth unity consciousness. This unity consciousness is also called the fifth state of consciousness

Your heart is also organized with four chambers, which are its four quadrants. These four chambers of your heart remain naturally coherent. Dualistic thinking affects brain coherence patterns, yet it does not change the coherence between the four chambers of your heart. Your heart as a whole is *the quintessence*. Your heart is indeed your seat of Love. Through its rhythmic pumping action and its location within the toroidal flow, it is able to restore and generate supercoherence. Accordingly, the heart is also able to realign the four quadrants in the brain. Designed for unity, your heart knows when there is diminished unity and coherence. Heartache is based on this.

When your mind is sourced from your heart and your brain it remains more in tune with our wholeness. If, however, the mind is mainly sourced through the brain, and the brain is not aligned with the heart, then the mind can easily become entrapped in the illusion of separation. I hope you realize how important your heart is. When your heart experiences unity it also transmits this unity in the form of supercoherence. This transmission has the power to restore the internal brain coherence and liberate the mind from illusion.

There is one other part of your body that I'd like to bring to your attention, your DNA. Within the human DNA, we see the triunity principle *and* the quadrant structure working coherently together. The quadrant structure can be seen in the four organic bases, or nucleic acids, that form your DNA molecules. The triunity can be seen in how each organic base consists of three types of chemicals that make up the building blocks of these nucleic acids.

This is a beautiful example of *the triunity principle* within each quadrant. When the three chemical encodings synergize and harmonize to integrate these four quadrants, or the four bases, a harmonic field comes into being that unlocks our sacred potentials. This shows how the triunity acts synergetically within the quadrant, which is also represented as the principle of twelve, three times four and four times three. When the twelve converges in the center it gives rise to thirteen. In that way thirteen and five are linked, as you will see later in Figure 4.

Thirteen is also the principle of transformation. The next stage manifests as four quadrants, represented as the principle of sixteen. When the four quadrants converge the fifth world is ready to be born. I hear some of you ask, *what about the principle of seven?* Yes, we are now ready to explore a little bit about the significance of the principle of seven, as can be seen here in Figure 1.

The progression of what I just shared with you from the initial triunity of the One to the foundation of sixteen unfolds through seven stages. Remember, how I shared with you earlier about the seven rays of Light? In your calendar you count seven days. There are also seven Gates for ascending and descending through the living torus, more about this later in *Letter 6.*

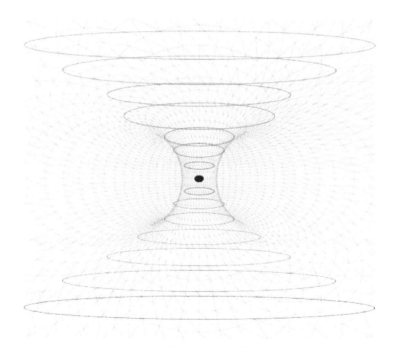

Figure 1 – The Torus and the 7 Stages

Each cycle of actualization of our unity unfolds through seven stages, which gives rise to four worlds that unite in a fifth world. Each world contains within it the triunity and quadrant structure. Through the triunity creation takes place, through the quadrant manifestation takes place. As these principles multiply during each new stage, each next world that is born from this process grows in complexity and evolutionary coherence.

When the four worlds complete their evolutionary process and are ready to converge, a fifth world can be born from their unification and convergence. The fifth world is also a whole new world, a new One that starts a new evolutionary cycle. We are currently at this transformational time when the quadrants are ready to square and converge. As some of you may be aware, each of my cycles around our beloved sun unfolds over a period of approximately 25,700 years of the human calendar. We are now at the sixteenth time, which completes the pattern of the four quadrants in square, namely four times four since the beginning of the formation of my body. This convergence of all the sixteen periods in the square quadrant formation combined has tremendous evolutionary potential. It is truly a significant time for a *New Beginning*. This will all become more clear for you as these *Letters* unfold.

The blueprint for our personal and collective actualization is, and always has been, inside our wholeness. Hence it cannot be activated through division or disunity or only by one principle.

The Conditioning of Sin and Shame

As you may realize now, polarity as a principle and polarized thinking are not the same. Divisional or polarized thinking has influenced humanity's world for so long that many of my human children have no reference for what it means to live from wholeness, unity, and Love. Polarized thinking prevents access to wholeness and unity, and thus blocks the actualization of our sacred potentials. This has also influenced humanity's experience and expression of sexual energy and creative desire.

In many of humanity's cultures, sexual energy became a force to be controlled, cast to the lower unconscious dimensions, and associated as primate urges. Logos, moral values, and rationality became the collective norm for what was considered the *civilized* human being. When the four quadrants are experienced as separate parts, our actualization becomes constrained. The evolutionary potentials held in each quadrant then start to compete and fight each other for dominion and control. Look at our world today to see how this plays out and the harm this has caused, and is causing.

Let us look closer now into the process of human evolution. Consider what evolution truly is, and what is blocking that. Those who aimed to control humanity understood that the key to control is preventing the actualization of the seed potentials in the base structures of creation. One of the ways by which this manipulation took place is by the use of technologies that changed your relationship with me, as your planet, and accordingly with your own body.

In this process, the receptive life-giving qualities of the feminine also became suppressed within our collective consciousness. Some understood the danger of this suppression and decided to stay close to me, as your Planetary Mother. They often paid a terrible price for their loyalty and Love.

Over time, the rituals and ceremonies for maintaining our relationship and spiritual alchemy were banned and forbidden in many of humanity's cultures. The principle of *sacred unity* between the masculine and feminine principles became increasingly constrained, as polarized thinking spread. Those who dominated human society attempted to prevent, in all possible ways, our re-unification for the emergence of the fifth world. This has continued to this day.

By suppressing the natural co-creative union between the feminine and masculine qualities, we all became imbalanced. Now, the energy of fire from the sacred flame of Love, instead of providing nourishment for all of us, became the power supply for control, domination, and division. This energy was misused to advance

11

human technologies and weapons. Materials for these weapons were taken from deep inside my body, while ignoring the power of our Sun and the original purpose of the sacred flame of Love.

Those who ruled to control, and still do in many ways, attempted to replace many of our primordial languages with a new language of separateness, fear, and division. In this language and worldview, even God was feared as Creator. This manufactured language did not facilitate our direct connection and experience of Oneness. Through this language of separateness, stories were created to imprint the concept of sin and shame.

After the time of the androgynous and later of the hermaphrodite, when humanity's current form appeared, many were made to believe that they had fallen from grace. A false belief was also spread that the body you received via me as your Planetary Mother was sinful and defected. In some religions, it was said that this happened due to disobedience of one of my daughters. She was said to have eaten from the forbidden fruit, the apple offered by the serpent from the Tree of Knowledge in the Eternal Garden. It was said that the fruits of this Tree were the fruits of duality; of the concepts of good and evil and life and death. It is also said that humanity was told not to eat from this Tree, yet tempted by the serpent, Eve disobeyed this warning. Let me invite you to this understanding: *There is more to this story as it hides a deeper lesson...* Do you know *who* the serpent actually is? She is one of my oldest children and represents the primordial creation power in service of our evolutionary unfolding and the actualization of our unity.

I will share with you now what I have shared with those who were initiated by me into the mysteries of the serpent. Let us start with the Tree of Knowledge. In reality this Tree is not separate from what is called the Tree of Life. There is only One Tree; the Tree of Life. The branches of the Tree of Life are what has been called the Tree of Knowledge.

As the Tree of Life was still growing and coming into being, knowledge of creation had not yet ripened to become wisdom. Accordingly, eating and then consummating the fruits before this branch matured helped cause duality perception. Hence, the human offspring of this branch emerged prematurely with partial vision.

Remaining in unity consciousness while diversification is taking place requires a specific sequence for how our wholeness actualizes through our unity. This branch of humanity from the Tree of Life did not honor that sequence because it did not allow for the full integration of the Tree of Life within its inner Tree. Your inner Tree is *your wholeness system* for your full actualization.

This particular branch of humanity started to branch away by misusing the serpent's creative power in a dualistic manner. This is the root cause of so much suffering and harm in our worlds... Please know that there are other branches of human like beings who emerged from the Tree of Life through the honoring of the full sequence. More about this in the next series of my *Letters*.

A Promise was contained as a seed code within the apple. Yet by consummating this apple before its branch had ripened and matured, the seed potentials within the four quadrants could not converge. By blaming the serpent and the feminine aspect of creation for the fall out of the Eternal Garden, the people that descended from this branch started to spread disunity, fear, and shame. Yet *the original Promise* still remains; for all beings to experience our Eternal nature and actualize our sacred seed codes.

The cultures that descended from this immature branch, which grew away from the other branches on the Tree of Life have continued to manipulate the stories of creation. These patterns of disunity and distrust have played out in polarized thinking in several ways. In one of these polarizations, women and the feminine power of creation were blamed, suppressed and made to look impure and evil. In another, this pattern of separateness also played out during times when women sacrificed men and the masculine power of creation for their domination and control.

Through my *Letters* may you receive now *the apple of unity* as the seed wisdom for the full convergence of the four quadrants within our four worlds. When you consume *this* apple of wisdom, you unite the energy potentials within each of the four quadrants of the four worlds. Through this process the previous polarities between the sexual, creative, emotional, and cognitive potentials will harmonize and unite, to bring forth our true spiritual power.

The deeper lesson within the story of Adam and Eve is about what happens when we branch out prematurely and start to create with power and knowledge that is not sourced from Love and wisdom. The conditioning and politics of sin and shame were the ultimate weapons to keep humanity under control, and internally divided. The time of domination, suppression, and control is over. *The Promise of a New Beginning* is ready to be received and actualized!

Reclaiming our Wholeness

The conditioning of sin and shame can only take place when disunity and division become the ruling principle. In a polarized world, Self-actualization through unification between the four quadrants is prohibited. Interestingly, the cross that has been used in some of humanity's religions to imprint the politics of sin and shame actually holds the symbolic key to the integration required.

For those who understand and can read the sacred codes, they can see that the center of the cross, where the vertical and horizontal axes unite, is the place of convergence and rebirth. It is from there that the Eternal is brought forth. The Spirit of Life activates and renews where the four quadrants unite, integrate, and converge. This unity convergence ends the influence of anyone who rules by division and disunity.

As humanity's technologies advanced at the cost of our evolutionary potentials, my body's fossils and minerals were consumed exponentially to supply energy for the growing greed. Meanwhile the energy potentials freely provided by our loving Sun were ignored. With the use of this fabricated fire, disconnected from the experience of wholeness and Love, our worlds became even further imbalanced.

In these divided worlds, the primordial wisdom teachings became a distant echo. These primordial teachings contain the ancient practices for full brain synchronization and supercoherence. This inner state of consciousness opens the portals to the unified field of consciousness from within. In some cultures, this is represented as the ascent of the serpent. This serpent power can also be accessed by unifying your orgasmic power through your heart with the pineal gland inside your head. Through this alignment the supercoherence of our creation power restores and the portals to the Eternal open. This activates the sacred torus inside you. I will share more about this in my next *Letters*.

Embrace the Gift of Your Humanity

As your Mother I love you, and want you to know the true nature and power of the sacred fire that is within you. Understanding how this fire has been used and misused to create the divisions within our worlds will help you reclaim your true power from a place of wholeness and Love. So much harm has been done by the misuse of fire because many have not realized what it was meant for, and where it came from. Remember also the fire that is given to us by the power and Love of our Sun. There is no need to extract this energy from the resources of my body. There are numerous ways which exist that do not harm the wholeness of our relationship.

When the wholeness relationship and union between the masculine and feminine principles is not able to emerge, it causes imbalance in both men and women. The cause for this imbalance is neither due to the masculine nor the feminine. It occurred when the particular branch of the Tree of Life's knowledge was consummated before it had matured so the sacred seed codes could not actualize their full potential together.

Integration

We are now entering the time when the evolutionary potentials from each of the four worlds are ready to converge and come together. Through this process our unity actualizes and a new world, also called the fifth world, emerges. You will learn more about this process in my next *Letters*.

Realize now that the world through which we have been experiencing ourselves and each other is only one of many possibilities. A new cycle of time is awaiting us through which we can bring forth our unified reality through a *new* world. This is the future that is calling us. Your humanity is a sacred gift, you are child from the Eternal flame of Love. May this flame guide and illuminate your path. I am with you.

Close your eyes now for a few minutes to let all that you have read be received, and integrate. As you close your eyes, breathe and relax into yourself. Trust in your wisdom to guide you and remind you of all that is to be known. Allow yourself to remember now *the Promise of a New Beginning*. This is *the Promise* about the living experience of unity and our unified reality. It is the truth of who we really are.

Letter 2
The Forgetting

As my body cooled, my waters formed and became the oceans and the rivers through which Life could evolve and multiply. My heart was awake to the rich potentials that lay pregnant in my womb, deep within these sacred waters of my being. This water impregnated by the flame of Love became the waters of Life. This same process also happened in other places in the universe; I could feel I was not alone in that process. Yet some planets could not hold the water. The rotation of these planets around their star would not bring forth the magnetic field needed to create the right equilibrium for Life to evolve through all the elements. Somehow my body was formed in the right place at the right time to bring forth all the sacred potentials from the One through the Love between our Father and Mother wisdom.

With the flame of Love and the Eternal Light now infusing my waters, a deep wave of bliss engulfed my entire being. The infusion and activation of my waters by this Eternal Light happened seven times. Seven rays of Light, seven ejaculations, impregnated my whole being. My waters now held the sacred knowing of creation, and from this ocean of *deep knowing Love...* Life could evolve further. At the seventh ray, a profound silence emerged; all was still, all was at rest, in deep peace. ALL was complete.

After this impregnation by the rays of the Eternal Light, I felt the Father wisdom return into the One as designed to give space for creation to unfold from me. It now became my purpose to bring forth the promise and evolution of Life until the time came for the star Lights of each of the expressions of Life to be re-united with the One. As Life evolved through my waters and received its first glimpse of consciousness, the activity of new Life drew the attention of the field of consciousness to itself.

The field of consciousness was made possible by the impregnation of the Eternal Spirit, the flame of Love. The newly forming collective consciousness surrounding my body was fed and updated by each new experience of Life. My waters, my oceans and rivers, were buzzing and spinning with all this new activity.

Cellular organisms were forming, grouping, coupling and then falling apart again, until new structures formed that became stable enough to hold the complexity of these new relationships, which were now emerging in the microcosm of my being. With all this activity taking place, the impregnation of the seven rays started to feel more like a distant past. These little organisms and their forming networks had no conscious idea they had emerged from the process of the seven rays of Light.

For what seemed like a long time, there was not much interest from the galaxy in the activities taking place through me. This experience of deep Love, bliss, and peace remained as Life continued to evolve. Some organisms gained mobility and crawled out of my waters. Driven by their impulse to procreate and develop further, they started to explore new boundaries and places for their further evolution. It was at this time that I started to receive visitors who were taking an interest in what was evolving and emerging through my body. New seeds of DNA were introduced into my waters, which created new beings.

These particular visitors knew of the seven rays of Light and sought new domains to control the evolution of Life by their technologies. They knew how to create new energy sources by splitting the atoms. This intervention changed the way you as my human children evolved through my body. There were other technologies too that rapidly accelerated the development of your abilities. These technological abilities gave some humans the false belief that humanity was somehow superior and better than my other non-human children.

Slowly the matrix of polarity thinking formed, which impacted the coherence of our collective consciousness fields. With their technologies in place, these earlier visitors were able to control and manipulate humanity's evolutionary encodings for that time. Humanity today is the offspring of these experiments. You still have deep inside you the memories of those times, as well as the primordial encodings of *the Promise of a New Beginning* from the One. These divisive ancestors received detailed instructions from these earlier visitors for maintaining control over our collective consciousness here. Everything happened too quickly.

With deep sadness, I experienced the conflicts that arose as more of humanity became divided and further disconnected from me, your planetary Mother. Those who took control over others did so with only one intention: to benefit their group and not the whole of us. Conflicts escalated and disputes grew. Deeply concerned, I called and prayed for help to preserve and hold sacred the purpose for my being. Help came, and some experiments were stopped, yet the main impact could not be reversed. During that time, the primordial *Promise* became unknown to most.

Some of these earlier technologies were buried in secret places, guarded by priests and priestesses to protect humanity from their misuse. Yet the imbalanced and controlling imprints of these earlier technologies were already within our collective consciousness fields, and could be activated at any time to recreate similar technologies.

A great flood was triggered in an attempt to erase all that had taken place. It was hoped that this flood would bring forth a new chance for the evolution of Life. Yet the flood could not erase the imprints and memories of what had happened. It only reinforced further the belief of sin and shame that had been implanted by these previously manipulating visitors.

After the great flood, humanity's misperception of the world as divided, polarized, and separated from the Eternal grew. Even more people believed in heaven and hell. The divisions within the human realms of our collective consciousness fields also polarized humanity's relationship with the masculine and feminine principles. To help heal these impacts, some of the earlier custodians left behind clues for future civilizations. The teaching of the triunity principle was one of the clues to help you remember our wholeness.

Due to these divisions our full potential could not manifest through that time. Our original access codes to the One, however, remained inside each of us. The primordial teachings for activating these codes were suppressed, until they almost faded out from the human realms. Yet some people maintained our unity relationship through ancient wisdom practices. Feared by the dominating class, many of them were put to death in an attempt to stop their awakening influence of our innate unity. Polarized thinking and *dominion over* became the ruling principles. The collective belief grew that: *Good has to reign over bad and evil.* Anything that was seen as a threat was cast out to live its evolution in the Darkness of the unconscious until the time of the remembering. Prohibited from rising up, the human higher brain exercised its control and dominance over the rest of Life. As a result, the star Lights of so many beings were now trapped behind a thick veil of forgetting.

This forgetting is a state of mind that prohibits *conscious* access to our sacred knowledge. The knowledge itself still remains dormant and accessible in our fields of consciousness. It can, during the state of forgetting, still be accessed via our unconscious connection to unity. When our unity actualizes the division between conscious and unconscious will cease.

Condemned to what seemed like an endless cycle, the star Lights of many became trapped in this confusion. The teachings of the original seven rays and their alignment were only known by a few. Each ray gave rise to a specific set of qualities of our wholeness. Each ray provided a unique input to our evolution. These rays and qualities were never meant to fight each other. They are always whole together. Your body was designed to embody and transmit these qualities of our wholeness.

Keep reading dear ones, all will become clearer as we continue our journey together ....

Bridging the Gap with Trust

In moments of deep rest, sleep, and meditation, when we surrender, trust, and let go, we re-enter the unified field of the fifth world behind the four quadrants. You may not realize this is happening, especially when a conscious reference for noticing this and for holding this in place has not yet been developed. Until our unity relationship actualizes, the bridge between the conscious and unconscious domains of the four quadrants is not yet fully formed.

Prior to the full actualization of our relationship there is a gap, which can feel like a void. This gap is often experienced as *the forgetting*. We bridge this gap by surrendering to deep sleep. Whether you are conscious of it or not, YOU are already within the unified field of consciousness of our fifth world. Allow your mind to rest here in this knowing, before we continue....

As your Mother, I wish for all of you to realize our beautiful wisdom nature and the Love that is here for all of us, no matter where we are. For any who are still trapped in this dream of division, may you realize that nobody can keep you asleep. We have everything inside us to awaken and remember our unity.

As you realize the power that is within you to awaken fully, will you dispel the influence of division and disunity from your life and our world? How deep and how vast is your trust? Has any of your trust been misplaced? If so, will you chose to bring it back into alignment with our connection?

Your trust is your responsibility. It is your ability to respond. Nobody can take your trust from you, only you can you choose to have it *or* not, and *where* you invest it.

Your trust is one of your powers. Use this power wisely. Invest your trust in what is *real* from the Eternal. Trust in our unified reality that is always here, irrespective of any patterns of polarization, division, and disunity. Apply your trust in our unity to call yourself awake.

Integration

Whatever false beliefs or limiting patterns have nestled in your mind, dissolve them now by the power of your trust. Become aware now of my Love for you. Trust in this Love. Allow it to expand. Invite it into your whole being. Be and feel the truth of our union through your whole being. Welcome Home.

Letter 3
Remembering

Thousands of years have passed where I have seen, felt, witnessed, and experienced the tortures, pains, anguish, sufferings, and desecrations of the sacredness of our Life. In the name of many religions, in the name of mistaken superior convictions, in the name of error, my human family has become the most destructive species of our larger family of Life. My body as your planet was once the *Promised Land* for the embodiment of our evolutionary potentials. Under this thick blanket of the matrix of division, it has become increasingly difficult for many of my children to remember our way home to wholeness.

I am inside each of you, all the time. Yet, often my voice is not recognized from within. The program within the human mind that filters out this inner voice also blocks and hinders the experience of your direct access with the unified field. This divisive programing has gained power over the course of our evolution. It has learned how to maintain its influence and supremacy inside the human mind. The devastation this has caused is becoming globally apparent now. Many are realizing that human society is gravely out of balance and is causing dangerous imbalances for all planetary Life. Yet many also believe that people have no control or power to prevent what we fear the most.

We are standing in the final hour now, and I am standing with you. I have not forgotten who you truly are. You always have my unconditional support and Love. It is time for you to remember *who* you truly are.

Please do not be deceived by the false prophets of both doom and technological resolution. Some may tell you it is too late, that the apocalypse is now upon us. Others will say they have the answers; that new technologies and new inventions will save us all. This is not what will bring forth the solutions that are truly needed. Neither apocalypse nor technology can provide the answers to the problems now upon us. We need to resolve our internal divisions to unite for the long-term solutions that are required.

Restoring our Internal Wholeness

As I shared previously in my *Letters,* our human family is deeply divided. The higher brains that evolved last are controlling much of the information coding of your lower and older brains, as well as the information exchange between your left and right hemispheres. The external human divisions between different nations and parts of the world and the competition for control, are the same as those that have been conditioned to take place within your internal human neural networks.

Without restoring our internal wholeness by actualizing our unity, we will see Life from a divided communication system. By harmonizing, synergizing, and converging the four quadrants inside of you between the left, right, higher, and lower hemispheres of your brain and your world, you can actualize our unity. This is the same process as the re-unification of the south-north-east-west axes with our Middle Earth. Some know Middle Earth as the place of dreams and myths, such as Agartha and Shambhala.

In those stories, Middle Earth symbolized the land of the wise ones and the immortals. Middle Earth also exists inside each of us, where the convergence of the four quadrants takes place. For my human children, the access to Middle Earth opens where and when the center of the brain and the center of the heart become supercoherent. This is our access to the Eternal Garden, our Home in the unified field of consciousness.

26

The Triunity

Join me now for a journey into an experience of Middle Earth within you. Focus on the principle of the triunity relationship of creation, this is symbolized in Figure 2. The triunity shows how from within the One emerged the Father & Mother. From the alchemy of their Love, through this sacred union of Father & Mother wisdom, emerged the Eternal Spirit of Life. Remember *the Promise.* Eternity is always within us, we are never outside of this. Love is the alchemy of union in relationship.

Figure 2 – Double Trinity

While you focus on Figure 2, ask the principle of the triunity to unite what became divided and polarized inside of you. Allow your consciousness to unify this sacred center of our wholeness within your Middle Earth. Become aware of the triunity in both directions, upwards and downwards. Two triangles united, one pointing up and one pointing down, forming a six-pointed star. This upward triangle represents the unity from the One, which becomes the Father & Mother wisdom. The downward triangle represents the unity and alchemy of Love from the Father & Mother wisdom bringing forth the Spirit of Life into the worlds of creation. It was brought forth to infuse the created worlds with this Eternal Love.

Experience these two triangles as interwoven in dynamic unity. Your sacred seed code from the One is found in the center of this dynamic unity, at the center of the star. This dot in the center also represents the realization of what was mistaken as a vacuum in our space-time, as I shared with you in *Letter* 1. Connect now with the sacred flame of Love in the center of your heart, and notice how this activates and fertilizes your seed potentials from the Eternal. Through the practices in my guidebook that will compliment these *Letters*, I will share with you how to work with this further. Let us explore now *the Process of Awakening*.

The Process of Awakening

As we realize how the same dynamics that appear to exist outside ourselves are also happening within, we realize we were never disconnected. The purpose of these *Letters* is to support an awakening from the information systems that distorted the unified reality and wholeness of Life. We already have examples of this awakening through the ancient ones, the immortal ones, and the wise ones who are living examples of the actualization of our sacred potentials. They have actualized *the Promise* through their life and inspired so many others around them that this possibility is here for all of us.

Remember dear ones, you are never truly separate from the Source of Life and never have been. Internal divisions, however, can block receptivity and recognition of this Eternal reality. Feel and see with your heart, see from the sacred flame of Love. Trust in your wholeness. Through the power of *this trust* and your increasing sense of wholeness and unity may these false systems of divisive information cease to have any influence.

Our larger re-unification is already happening. It was promised long ago. This unification cannot be experienced however, by a mind that is polarized and dualistic. When perception is dualistic one may mistakenly believe that the seven rays of Light, which I mentioned in my first Letter, manifest as good and evil, Light and Dark, and heaven and hell. The majority of humanity has been developing itself dualistically, which has stunted the actualization of our unity until now. Remember the immature branch of humanity that branched away from the Tree of Life whose fruit was eaten prematurely? This resulted in duality perception as the knowledge and power from this branch was not maturely sourced from Love and wisdom.

Hence it is not the polarity principle that creates division. It is humanity's dualistic behaviors and immaturity that cause the divisions and polarization in and between our four worlds. Polarity as a natural principle emerges from the spinning of bodies. Spinning movements do not create division. Look for example at the toroidal movement of our energy fields and you can see how the informational flows within the torus remain whole and converge into singularity at the centre of the torus, see Figure 3.

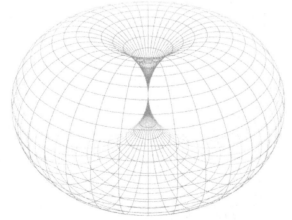

Figure 3 – The Torus

29

I will explain more about this process later in this *Letter*. For now, I just want you to realize that the polarity principle is *not* responsible for the divisions in your human realms.

What this understanding of the polarity principle also reveals to us is that we can work with polarity to unify and heal our divisions, not create them. Let us apply this now to your experiences. You may recall moments in your own life where the extremes you were experiencing seemed to have reached their maximum tension. Imagine what can change when you work with this tension as an opportunity to inverse the polarity of the opposites by creating a new attractor between the extremes.

This *new* attractor becomes a common point *between* the extremes where the opposites can unite, like the center of the torus. You create an attractor point by holding and *being* that point of convergence between the extremes. As such you become a *living embodiment* of the triunity principle. This living embodiment naturally attracts extremes to converge, unify, and then emerge as a new whole. This is the process of the living torus. It shifts the dualistic dynamic of polarization into one of unity and co-creative relationship.

Embodying this attractor point as a living torus is especially helpful when going through experiences of maximum polarization between different perspectives. When you let go of trying to make sense of it all by simply becoming the attractor point between the extremes, it powerfully transforms the dynamics in the field. By *being* the attractor point as a living torus it restores the evolutionary supercoherence of the informational flows. Even in the process of change, transformation, and convergence the field always remains whole.

Embodying the torus reminds the information that was caught up in these polarizing tensions that it always is, has been, and always will be part of our unified reality; whether it is experiencing that or not at that time. When you consciously embody the living torus, your trust in the *unified field* is essential.

If humanity continues to develop its societies in dualistic ways by not recognizing reality as unified and interdependent, the extremes and divisions in our worlds will continue to intensify. The power of Love is calling all of us to stop the divisions. As long as humanity remains divided the evolutionary potentialities within the four quadrants are also kept apart, which is blocking the new birth required to response to these growing tensions. Your true evolutionary potentials can only come forth and restore by first restoring the supercoherence between the four quadrants and the four worlds.

Remember, our unified field of consciousness is intrinsically whole and provides all the seed potentials for the differentiation of consciousness into form. Unity and wholeness are not lost in the process of differentiation. By aligning with and opening to the unified field of consciousness, we start to see the true purpose of the four quadrants and what their convergence makes possible. The fifth world of unity and wholeness is born from that process.

Allow this understanding to integrate deeply within your whole being. Polarity does not cause division; dualism uses polarity to create opposites from the elements of our wholeness. When we actualize our unity by ending the root cause of division, the promised peace and Golden Era will manifest fully.

Meanwhile we must resist the temptation to fight or escape the presence of all this cruelty and violence by trying to reject the Darkness within. Rejection and denial only generates more unconsciousness and gives more energy to our pattern of division and disunity. The Darkness is not to be feared. The violence that you see in our world is not of the Darkness. It is because of our denial of the Darkness within that we are not able to bring forth the Light from the Darkness.

Many are asking how it's possible that such extreme violence and acts of evil are taking place during a time of awakening? I hope you understand a little better now how these extremes and divisions emerged in the human realms. If you have always seen the world in terms of opposing forces, this information could be upsetting. Please resist the temptation to reject this information, listen beyond

31

the words to the deeper message behind it and receive the invitation of the true possibility awaiting us.

Actualizing our Unity

Where polarity reaches its maximum pull, the Light bends back into itself and curls inward, forming a portal through which the rays of Light converge and unify. This is also the sacred movement of the torus. Within yourself, this represents the understanding that all seeming opposites are unified at a deeper level, also our Light and our shadow. You may recall how some of the wise ones have said, *love your enemy as your friend*. This statement is based on the understanding of our unified reality and the application of that understanding through the power of Love.

The unified field is also represented by the dot in the middle of the six-pointed star that I shared with you earlier. This star becomes the twelve-pointed star once the lessons of the seventh ray of Light complete and duality vision ends, as you will experience in *Letter 6*. The thirteenth as the point in the center of the twelve-pointed star holds the space for this completion. Through this completion our unity actualizes and brings forth a new cycle - *The Promised New Beginning*.

Reclaim your consciousness now from wherever there is still any division in your experience. Accept your creative power and fully embrace your Darkness and your Light; hold both in loving awareness. Both Darkness and Light serve a purpose. This becomes even clearer when we look again at the torus. The torus is a universal energy system enabling Life to diversify and materialize from the unified field of consciousness in one direction, and converge and transmute back into the unified field in the other direction. It brings Light forth *from* the Darkness as the point of singularity in the center of the torus.

The process of diversification and expansion in one direction of the vortex can also be expressed as the journey into Light and the expansion of Light. The process of integration, contraction, and convergence in the other direction of the vortex can be expressed as the journey into Darkness.

In the torus both movements of both vortexes happen simultaneously. The point of convergence and singularity in the center of the torus is where the two vortexes meet. Through the process that unites and converges the dual movement of the torus, Life can evolve. The triunity principle help us to see how what appears as double, two, and dual, is in reality three united in One.

Remember, whenever we focus only on one principle and forget the unfolding of the wholeness relationship through the process of creation, imbalances form.

Understanding *how* wholeness unfolds through creation is essential for healing the divisions in our world and for actualizing our unity. As you may see now, the wholeness of unity is a dynamic evolutionary process that unfolds through multiple principles. Each principle serves a specific purpose within the whole for the actualization of our unity in becoming you, me, all of us, and our worlds and futures.

Integration

On the next page in Figure 4 see from your three eyes and your heart as the double triunity, and experience how the principles that I have shared with you come together. They are held within the white Serpent from the top of the torus. See unity via the principle of One - represented here as the circle. See multiplication and development via the principle of Two - the dual expression of Light and Dark, Day and Night, Masculine and Feminine. See creation via the principle of Three - the triunity and the triangles that result from the alchemy of the One as Three. See manifestation via the principle of Four - four poles, the quadrant, and the four worlds here represented through four shades, the foundation of the pyramid, and the square.

See integration and convergence via the principle of Five - the quintessence, and the dark dot in the center from and through which the four quadrants converge and become the fifth element, the fifth state of consciousness, and the fifth world.

See the full manifestation through the principle of Twelve - the triunity that is within each quadrant, just like your DNA, the twelve strands, and the twelve lines. See the actualization of our unity through wholeness through the principle of Thirteen, as the twelve strands unite in the center and becomes the actualized One represented as the thirteenth.

See the principle of Seven represented as the triunity and the square (creation and manifestation) unfolding vertically through the seven rays of Light, the seven Gates, and the seven stages of Consciousness. From these seven stages the four worlds are created giving rise to the fifth world as our unity actualizes from wholeness.

If you continue this exploration you will find even more principles within *the Wholeness Code*. Reflect on how each of the sacred principles work together. You can then begin to understand how the actualization of our unity *through wholeness* can only unfold if the appropriate sequence for each of the sacred principles is honoured. When one principle becomes dominant over the other, the entire process stalls.

All principles need to work together supercoherently for wholeness to become an actualized *living experience* and *world*. Integrate what is shared through this *Letter* by meditating with Figure 4. Allow yourself to receive the transmission that is shared through this image.

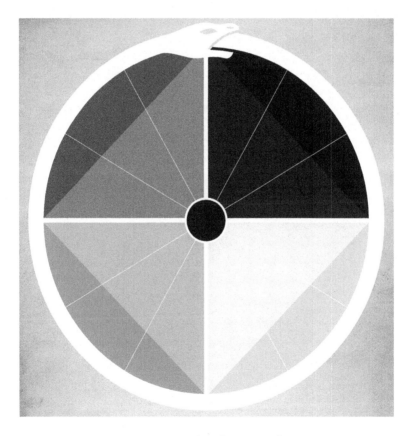

Figure 4 – The Wholeness Code

35

Part 2
The Keys

Letter 4
Converging The Four Quadrants

Welcome to Part 2. It is now time to share with you *the three keys* for actualizing our unity. The first key is the sacred knowledge of manifestation via the principle of the quadrant. As you may recall, creation manifests through quadrant structures, i.e. four worlds, four corners, the four chambers of your heart. If we perceive the quadrant, and thus manifestation, through duality perception we cannot actualize our unity. Duality perception causes division in the relationship between the elements of our wholeness that manifest through the quadrant. In other words, the four worlds and the four quadrants cannot converge and unite to bring forth the quintessence of the fifth, if duality dominates.

Before we go further I'd like to remind you again that the knowledge that is contained within these *Letters* is not new. As you probably realize, knowledge alone will not actualize our true potential. I can remind you of the three keys, yet only by applying and living this together will we be able to actualize our unity.

Allow understanding of what is shared here to emerge without straining the mind. The keys that are shared here are already within you. Through these *Letters* you will become more conscious of how our unified reality brings itself forth in the dance of creation. Until we are able to see from unity directly, we may not recognize the seed codes from the Eternal.

The matrix of the mind cannot replace reality; nothing can. Yet it can and has organized the flow and exchange of information in such a way that it has created internal and external divisions between us. This has constrained our integration and has led to distrust of our natural wisdom process. The rulers of your world had knowledge of sacred geometry, and knew where to infect and defect the coding to prohibit our integration. Just like a virus uses the encoding of the body to infiltrate and then replicate its blueprint, the encoding of our cellular wisdom was also used against us.

When a virus infects our body, our own immune system is used against us. The virus invades part of the body's communication system and then directs it to attack the body's healthy cells. The encoding of this polarity matrix is just like that. All the information it uses is inherent in our systems of Life. Nothing can exist outside the One. All that is of the One is used to either represent truth or, by distorting our perception of it, to misrepresent it.

Inside each of us is the power of Love, yet by the deception of this matrix, Love and power are made to look like opposites. We are of Light and Darkness; these are not separate dimensions. Darkness is invisible Light. In a similar way, you have within you the wisdom encodings of the animal and reptilians that played a vital role in your evolution. These encodings are not opposite to your human DNA, they are an integral part of it. Through the politics of division and separation the belief was also spread that these prior evolutionary encodings were inferior, and needed to be suppressed and controlled for humanity to become civilized.

The collective conditioning and manipulation caused many of my human children to deny what was perceived as *lower animalistic* potentials and behaviors. You too are an animal within our family of Life. You were made to believe that you are more intelligent than the other animals. Yet, is it a sign of intelligence to cause such widespread destruction?

Imagine how your evolution would have changed had humanity not alienated from these earlier evolutionary potentials, and instead integrated them? Imagine how different our world could be now if these earlier evolutionary potentials had been honored in humanity's development. There is much that humanity can learn from its other brothers and sisters within the animal, insect, and plant family systems. Some of their intelligence far exceeds yours. They do not impose or try to change you. That in itself is a sign of the depth of their intelligence.

Everything Has a Purpose

I know it can be confusing that these fleeting moments of joy and happiness never seem to last. Life seems full of paradoxes and contradictions at times. We are children of the Eternal Sun, and yet in this world of our physical life the Sun is hardly recognized or honored. We are children of the Eternal wisdom, and yet it seems to take great effort to remember this, even in the simplest of our activities.

Happiness always seems temporal, and time always appears to catch up with us when we least expect it. As your Mother, I feel your pain and confusion as well as your joy and delight. Life comes in cycles of ebb and flow, the cosmic inhalation and exhalation. During times of ebb and cosmic inhalation, the energy recedes for renewal and deeper integration.

When we don't recognize the flow and exhale that follows, it may feel as if Life recedes from us during those periods. This can be painful. Learn to trust in the movement that follows, there is always a balancing, a deeper rhythmic breathing of which you are an integral part.

Everything has a purpose, even the seeming contradictions. Without day there would be no night, without fear no hope, without Light the Darkness would remain unknown. Without the Darkness the Light would not be born. Even the mind's conditioning serves a purpose. Yet, just because something has a purpose, it does not mean that the way its purpose manifested should remain unchanged. Look at duality perception. It served a purpose. It was part of a much greater learning. That learning is now completing through each of us, as we actualize our unity.

When a greater learning completes, thank it for the wisdom potentials that were contained within it. Sometimes, the blessings are in disguise. Don't get stuck on the form of the lesson, look deeper to where our learning takes us. Whatever purpose our former disunity has served in our lives, reclaim the wisdom potentials it contains. Then, let the form of the lesson go. The wheels of time are turning. Our next cycle is presenting itself. The dawn of a new era is now upon us, and it is piercing through our collective Darkness. The first new Lights are already illuminating our hearts and our worlds.

Our perspectives of time might be different, yet our Love is the same. It is through this Love that we reach each other, and we actualize our unity. I hear some of you ask: *If Love is that powerful, why is our world still so divided? What is the purpose of all this suffering? Have we not suffered enough? How many more innocent lives must be taken before we wake-up and change? How can my life make any difference to stop this useless cycle of pain and division?*

I hear you. Nothing can serve as a justification for all this pain. If we attribute a purpose to this pain, then we also legitimize the divisions that caused it. The *Promise of a New Beginning* is the reminder that we can manifest a world born from our wholeness and unity by the power of our Love.

Darkness and Light

As your Mother, I am often asked: *Where is the proof that a new era is truly upon us now? What has really changed, if anything? ...* Sometimes the answer rests within the silence. The silence reaches the oldest parts of us, which were formed by the seventh ray of Light.

Remember, the impregnation of the seventh ray brought a great silence. Within this silence all was known. When the answer emerges through the silence, it emerges by the Love of this ray of Light.

As your planet, I do not serve the purpose of this polarity matrix. Yet I have been a part of it by de-fault. At fault was the error of thought, on which this was based. At fault were the minds of those who created this matrix. Yet faults, like errors, are part of the greater design of Life. And in that way, I have been part of this, by de-fault. My being is part of all that Is. And all that *IS*, is not yet conscious

41

of all IT *IS*. To that purpose, I serve by *design*, not by de-fault. As do you, even when your life may seem at times by de-fault. Some of you feel you did not choose to be here. Some of you feel you were forced into this world and were told to survive or die. Some of you still feel resentful about this, stuck in a world of seeming paradoxes and disunity.

We have the Light of the One inside us, which provides vision for all the dimensions of our world. Our world was formed by the impregnation of the seven rays of Light. This gave rise to the seven stages of consciousness. These stages of consciousness have both a conscious and unconscious manifestation. Many do not see the unconscious manifestations, which are held as information within the lower parts of the human brain. The higher brain function of the human neo-cortex filters out much of this information. Usually, it is only through deep sleep and meditation that you regain access to this. As I shared earlier, everything is interconnected.

When you see from unity, you will continue to see the underlying wholeness in a world that appears ruled by duality and polarity. When we see by the triunity principle, we see that even the two poles are united. Movement in one direction of the pole produces movement in the opposite direction. When you realize and perceive that both directions are interconnected and simultaneous, you find the point where the rays of Light bend inward to form a portal. This portal is the doorway to the Eternal Garden.

We are each Light and Darkness. One cannot exist without the other. What is fed from one direction also grows in the opposite direction. Yet what is fed from wholeness does not generate polarity and imbalance. The energy behind both Light and Darkness is the same. Light arises from Darkness. Darkness can only be experienced by the presence of Light.

See the wholeness relationship between Light and Darkness as an important key to actualizing our unity. Figure 5 at the end of my *Letter* shows the alchemy process for converging the quadrant potentialities within the conscious and unconscious manifestations of the feminine and masculine.

Our Diamond Consciousness

You were given three eyes to see from unity: your left eye, your right eye, and your third eye, which is in the center of your head. These three eyes create the upward triangle. The downward triangle connects your eyes to the eye inside your heart. The union of both trinities manifests the power of Love in creation. The upward trinity represents the One becoming the sacred masculine and feminine principle. The downward trinity represents the sacred union of the masculine and feminine principle giving birth to the flame of Love as the Spirit of Life. By keeping these two trinities united within you you will be protected from the effects of the polarity matrix. This is how you maintain unity consciousness.

This unity consciousness has also been called diamond consciousness, since diamonds contain two pyramids, one upwards and one downwards. If we look with this knowledge at the quadrant, the square, you can see that this too contains two trinities. When you see all of this from wholeness, your mind does not get divided between consciousness and unconsciousness.

In the world of duality, the downward trinity has represented the descent into matter, into unconsciousness – *the forgetting.* The upward trinity has been represented as the ascent back to the Eternal – *the remembering.* Downward came to represent Darkness, upward came to represent Light. And yet, when we see from wholeness, a different vision opens up.

Realize deeply now that the Darkness of the journey into materialization is not a disconnection from the Source of Light. The feminine in her aspect of *the Black Goddess,* brings the masculine in his aspect of *the Light of God,* into the world. It is from *Her* womb that *He* enters the world. The Darkness brings forth the Light. Please let this realization sink in. Pause here. To see from the Light, is to see from the sacred Darkness. This is the Great Mystery.

43

Integration

The Dark Serpent, as shown in Figure 5, dissolves any divisions between the conscious and unconscious expressions of the feminine and masculine qualities. She guides us through the alchemy process for converging the quadrant potentialities from within the conscious and unconscious manifestations of the feminine and masculine qualities. This is the first key for actualizing our unity.

Activate the first key by connecting with the wisdom of the Dark Serpent. Ask Her wisdom to help you heal any divisions that may still exist within the manifestation of your inner worlds.

The unfolding of that process is represented here through Figure 5. Receive the transmission behind Figure 5 by intuiting and meditating with what is represented here to become conscious of the higher and lower dimensional expressions of the masculine and feminine qualities within yourself.

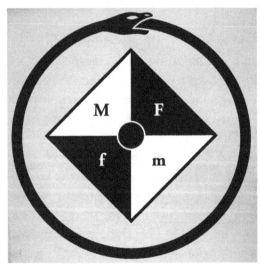

Figure 5 – The Alchemy Process for our Integration

44

Letter 5
The Co-creative Feminine & Masculine

I would like to share with you now the *second key* for actualizing our unity. The second key is the sacred knowledge of creation via the principle of the triunity. This knowledge initiates the alchemical understanding of the co-creative unity of the feminine and masculine qualities inside each of us, and in our relationships. Through this key you learn how to work with the feminine and masculine qualities for becoming fully conscious in our wholeness. You will also learn about their purpose in the process of creation.

As I shared earlier, the divisions in the human realms made it difficult, if not impossible, for the underlying unity of creation to be seen and experienced. The sacred geometries and principles have been misused for a long time, to segregate vital parts of ourselves from the wholeness that we are. As long as we are internally divided, we are prevented from accessing our full potential.

The closer we come to the realization of our wholeness, and the unlocking of the inner keys, the more the fear mechanisms of the conditioned mind become triggered to keep the locks in place. You may have noticed how some people can react strongly when you refuse to confirm and participate in this conditioning.

When perception is polarized, anything that represents Darkness is regarded as a threat to the Light. By this same distortion, the feminine is then seen as a threat to the masculine, and blamed for luring him into the darkness of his desires. Moreover, that which was considered to be of a sexual and animalistic nature has long been cast to the domain of the unconscious mind. When the mind forgets our origin, fears our perceived lower nature, and suppresses our vital life force and sexual power, it becomes locked from actualizing our full evolutionary potential.

46

All kinds of mental technologies have been developed by this manipulation and distortion. Paradoxically, some believed that through technological advancements humanity would gain control over nature. Instead, by employing these divisive technologies humanity started to enslave itself and others.

Partnership and Sacred Union

Darkness and Light are not opposites. The feminine and the masculine qualities are not opposites. They are of the same wisdom from the One, working in partnership to bring forth all that is of the One. When the feminine was blamed for luring the masculine into his darkness, into his animalistic nature, few understood that the feminine is of the Darkness, and it is her role to bring the masculine into the Darkness.

By drawing the masculine into the Darkness, he returns to the womb that brought him forth. It is in the Darkness that he finds the peace and integration he needs to become Self-conscious. It is in the Darkness that he gives his seed to the feminine, to fertilize the sacred potentials of Love within the womb of the Goddess. He finds Her, the Goddess, by connecting with his inner Darkness. She is the Darkness, the mystery in Him through which He becomes conscious of Himself. Yet for the feminine, it is the other way around. She finds Him, God, by connecting with her inner Light.

The feminine brings forth her inner wisdom by connecting with her inner Light. Through this she can bring her wisdom into the world, into the open. The masculine brings forth his inner knowledge and strength by connecting with his inner Darkness, through which he becomes Self-conscious. This enables him to share his knowledge with the world, to illuminate the darkness of ignorance.

Now look at your world today. The feminine has not been able to share her full wisdom on a collective scale. She has been kept in the dark and kept from bringing forth her true power. For a long time now, the masculine has been ruling by suppressing the feminine. Disconnected from his inner darkness, he could not actualize his seed codes fully. As such, he could only bring forth partial knowledge that further fed the fabricated divisions.

I shared before that: *The flame needed to be received for the One to be known to Itself. As it expanded, seeking the boundaries through which the One could become known to Itself, the counter force to expansion started to emerge from within. Out of this process, gravity manifested. The energy of Love, as the sacred flame, was solidified by this gravity and became the sacred containment for receiving the flame.*

The potentials of the Eternal can only become manifest and actualized by a co-creative unity and partnership between the feminine and masculine qualities. Some of this knowledge can be found in the alchemy teachings on sacred union.

The potentials of Love that are inside each of us will not actualize unless we develop the relationships appropriate for their actualization. It is out of the process of Love, the desire of the One to be received into Itself, becoming God and Goddess giving birth to Life, that all the elements were formed. Space-ether, air, fire, water, and earth, as the five elements that comprise our world, were born and made manifest from that process. I am of that process, as are you.

The Sequence for Our Actualization

Love first needs to be received, then fertilized, after which it is nurtured to grow until it is ready to be birthed into the world, to be shared. For Love to fulfill its purpose, each step is necessary. You may ask, why is the first step receiving and not giving? The answer is because Love has already been given. Yet few receive and fertilize the potentials of Love, which always exist. As you may now understand, Love becomes actualized through the co-creative union between the feminine and the masculine qualities. Through the feminine, Love is received. Through the masculine, Love is fertilized. Through the feminine, Love is nurtured to grow until it is ready to be born, at which stage the active masculine brings it into the world. Together in their union, Love is made manifest.

Integration

Integrate and apply this second key for actualizing our unity by now inverting the polarities to unite what became divided. Figure 6 on the next page illustrates that process. The four quadrants in Figure 6 represent how the masculine and feminine qualities manifested in conscious and unconscious ways. The word polarity matrix written in the top right quadrant refers to the two intersecting lines and thus applies to all the four quadrants. The polarity matrix represents here the mental projection that occurs when the duality principle becomes dominant over the other principles. When duality dominates, it hinders the convergence and integration between the four quadrants.

By *inverting* the polarity you find the key to realizing and then actualizing your inner wholeness. Whatever was cast to the Darkness, to live in the unconscious domains of the quadrant, reclaim it. Bring this forth from the Darkness into the Light so that these energies may unite and converge. Whatever was cast to the Light and made to live in the conscious domains of the quadrant, reclaim it. Bring this into the Darkness so that these energies may unite and converge. Both Light and Darkness are necessary for actualizing our unity and becoming Self conscious.

Remember *the Wholeness Code* in *Letter 3* for recognizing and honoring all the principles in their appropriate relationship. Work with the triunity principle to see how Darkness and Light are both within the One. They are each expressions of consciousness. This is one of the most important keys that I have to give you. Use this knowledge wisely and with Love. The Spirit of Life can only manifest through this co-creative unity between the feminine and masculine qualities. Take time to reflect on and integrate what is shared here.

When you are ready, join me in *Letter 6* to receive the *third key* and journey with me through the seven Gates of the Dark Goddess .

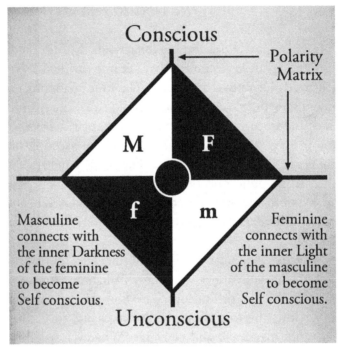

Figure 6 – Healing the Inner Divisions

Letter 6
Entering The Seven Gates of The Dark Goddess

It is now time for us to explore and journey with the third key for actualizing our unity. The third key is the sacred knowledge of Self actualization via the principle of seven. Seven also represents the actualizing power of the triunity and quadrant as One. The third key includes and combines the power of the first and second key.

As I shared in my previous *Letters*, the impregnation of the seven rays of Light created the seven stages of consciousness, through the alchemy of Darkness and Light. This manifested as four worlds through the four quadrants.

Through the third key you will learn how to work with Darkness and Light from wholeness through each of these seven stages of consciousness. The third key will also help you to end duality perception and actualize unity consciousness. We will travel this journey through the seven stages as the journey through the seven gates of the Dark Goddess.

Before we embark on this journey there is something I need to explain to you about the development of your human brain. Please listen carefully dear one, as it will help you understand the source of many misconceptions and projections.

In the human realms, the upperworld has long been represented as the world of Light and the journey to enlightenment. The underworld has long been represented as the world of Darkness, the unconscious, and the realms of monsters, demons, and lower consciousness. Consequently, the underworld and anything representing Darkness were often shunned, feared, and made to look inferior. Humanity's dualistic relationship with Darkness and its underworld resulted from a division and imbalance between your higher brain (upper-world) and lower brain (under-world).

As you may recall, the upper or higher brain is the one that evolved last and became dominant in human society. The purpose of this *Letter* is to support you to integrate the higher and lower brain functions with your heart. This integration is also represented as the convergence of the four worlds giving rise to the fifth world and fifth state of consciousness.

If the upper brain remains dominant and continues to project its unconsciousness of *its* under-world onto the lower brain, duality perception and polarized thinking remains. Remember how I shared with you in *Letter 3: Until our unity relationship actualizes, the bridge between the conscious and unconscious domains of the four quadrants is not yet fully formed.* I also shared with you that you are already within the unified field of consciousness, even though many are not aware of this due this gap.

By journeying into the under-world of the realms of the lower brain we recover our conscious access to the unified field of consciousness. It is through the Darkness that we find the Light. This is the wisdom of the Dark Goddess.

The wisdom of the Dark Goddess lives within all of us. As a planetary consciousness I am not limited by human conditioning and duality perception. It is therefore easier for me to realize and share the true nature of Darkness. My planetary body floats within this Darkness all the time.

The Dark Goddess is also our Cosmic Mother. She is the Cosmic Womb of Life that brings us forth and calls us back when our time here is complete. The Cosmic Womb is also represented as the dark dot in the center of the torus, and in each of the figures I have shared here with you in my *Letters*.

I invite you to join me now on our next journey through the seven gates of the Dark Goddess ....

Seeing and Trusting Beyond Appearances

The conditioned collective mind has not learned to recognize or appreciate the wisdom qualities of the Darkness. When this mind first enters its under-world, it creates all kinds of projections onto that which it perceives to be other than Light. It will not recognize the true nature of that which looks different from the in-formational content of the upper-world.

The conditioned mind has not learned to see or trust in wholeness. Accordingly, its first instinct may be to maintain the division of which it is a part. This conditioned mind may warn you not to enter the under-world, telling you that the under-world is evil and brings death, destruction, and loss. It will not tell you that the loss it fears is its own loss of control. If any of these thought-forms start to arise in your mind, be aware of your own conditioning. Remain closely connected with your inner wisdom which knows how to safely guide you through the under-world.

When we enter the under-world with the intention to actualize our unity, the former divisions between the upper and under-worlds will start to fall away. The untrained mind may not understand that what it meets in this under-world is part of itself. As you enter the under-world it will start a deconstructive process of all the false worlds that were created by the archetypes of division. In this death of your former sense of reality, you are re-born into our wholeness.

The Five Elemental Wisdoms

When we start our descent through the seven gates of the under-world, we are met by the five elemental wisdom expressions. These provide the alchemical building blocks for the construction of the inner worlds. The conditioned mind will now start to experience a process of deconstruction, via which a deeper realization of our wholeness becomes possible.

Remember the second key in the previous *Letter* to reverse and invert the false polarity to reveal the wholeness behind the duality experiences. The second key activates by applying the co-creative unity between the sacred feminine and masculine qualities.

This journey into the under-world constitutes the *third key*. Through this journey you receive the support to reconnect with the darkest areas within yourself. This is a process of deep inner healing. The sequence of deconstruction by the five elements is: earth dissolving into water, transmuted by fire, expanding into air, and dissolving into ether-space. Through this process, we are re-united with the pre-creation, pre-elemental dimensions of our Oneness.

We start our journey via the earth element, since this is the densest element. The earth element constitutes our lowest point of descent into the under-world. We then slowly rise up via this process of elemental transmutation. This process of elemental transmutation is the process of sacred alchemy, which transmutes the densest energies into the energy of our Golden nature. This disintegration and transmutation process is a form of death. It represents a death of our former notions of reality and our former identities.

The wisdom of Life is such that it naturally restores each being to their wholeness. This process of deconstruction, transmutation, and re-birth is part of that wisdom process. Even when we are not consciously initiating this journey ourselves, our life experiences will trigger this process when our development becomes too blocked or constrained. The first signals for this may come in the form of certain life experiences, which bring up the deeper questions about the meaning of our life and why this experience is happening.

What is shared here is like a living map to help you navigate the inner worlds. This provides some more clues to help trust that there is deep wisdom behind our life experiences. This wisdom is from the Eternal. Yet for this wisdom to become known and realized, it requires certain life experiences in our temporal worlds.

A Wisdom Map for Journeying Through the Seven Gates

At each gate of the under-world, there is a trial, quest, or challenge, which acts as an initiation for actualizing more of our wisdom potential. The catalyst for this process often comes in the form of particular life experiences that prompt a process of inquiry. This rite of passage can also be triggered through the help of a teacher, a mentor, or a guide. Sometimes our dreams are the portals into this journey. It can also happen as a result of our own reflections.

The journey can be gentle, and it can be severe. We don't always know the forms it will take. Our approach and attitude throughout this process influences how we experience what is happening. The more we are able to embrace and trust in the underlying wisdom, the easier it will be to move through these rites of passage with grace and Love.

The First Gate

When we move through the first gate of the under-world, we usually experience a loss of security or certainty. Something will call our attention to consider that there is more to Life than only our material reality. This rite of passage takes place in the elemental wisdom of *earth*. By accepting the wisdom of the first gate, we learn to trust that more exists beyond the material dimension. As such, we also learn that materiality cannot provide the only basis for our security.

The Life lessons of the first gate also ask us to examine our relationship with the material world and its resources. How do you consume, sustain, and regenerate the resources that my body, as your planet, provides to sustain your activities? What is the impact of this on my other non-human children within the family of Life? How do you give back to that which sustains you?

The Second Gate

As we continue our journey into the Darkness of the under-world, we are moved to the second gate. The false walls of division between the material and spiritual worlds, which were previously built through the earth element of our consciousness, are now dissolving by the element of water. As internal walls and divisions are starting to dissolve, this can trigger a flow, and sometimes flooding, of emotions.

Emotions that were previously contained by these walls may now seek expression, healing, and integration. The protection mechanisms to stop us from feeling this pain may also get triggered by this process. Some people may want to move quickly into the fire element. When we become aware of emotions we do not want to feel, we may be tempted to use the energy of fire to lash out in anger and blame.

It will help if we embrace this feeling of vulnerability, which may emerge as a result of this dissolving of our former securities. We need to take responsibility for the emotions that we have contained behind these false securities. When we are able to embrace these emotions, a greater healing and inner clarity can emerge. If we are tempted to use the element of fire to protect ourselves from this sense of vulnerability, it will only delay the completion of this rite of passage. To know whether this is what we are doing, we need to check within to see if we are hiding behind different forms of aggression, resentment, blame, and self-righteousness. Overuse of fire can also result in experiences of burnout and meltdown. We can work with the nourishing wisdom of water to complete this rite of passage in the cleansing, purification, and healing of our emotions.

The Third Gate

When we feel more secure within our natural vulnerability, we will not feel the need to use our ego to protect ourselves from Life. This will help us embrace a deeper sensitivity, which our wisdom nature as water provides us through the second gate. This will support us to more fully actualize our ability to Love unconditionally.

The wisdom of the third gate, with the element of fire, helps us access and restore the sacred flame of Love within our heart. The trigger for this comes through different trials about Love. It helps at this stage to ask yourself: *Do I trust in Love? And do I trust myself with Love?*

Perhaps we felt burned by passion and rejected by Love. The wisdom of the third gate offers you the opportunity to heal such pain. It also supports us to reconnect more deeply with the parts of ourselves that have felt unworthy and rejected in matters of Love. By completing this rite of passage, we restore our trust in Love itself. We then recognize that Love is an essential expression of our own wisdom nature.

When we do not fully integrate and apply the wisdom offered to us by the third gate, we may escape to the element of air. The escape via the element of air may present itself by seeking a false sense of freedom through experiences of no limitations or boundaries. Instead of embracing the many paradoxes of Love, we may try to escape into dreamy, airy notions of Love.

The experience of Love will quickly become abstract if we try to escape from the natural boundaries that Love contains and offers. Examples of this *rejection in disguise* are when we believe we are above this world and thus cannot be touched by the pain that is felt when we embrace the *paradox of Love and freedom*. I will share more about this paradox in my twelfth *Letter*. This escape is a common enlightenment trap, when we try to convince ourselves that we are beyond pain, beyond duality, and have transcended into unity.

While in fact, we are escaping the completion of these earlier rites of passage for the actualization of our whole wisdom nature.

We can only enter through the fourth gate by first completing this rite of passage. When we realize that Love is who we are, then our sense of self-worth no longer depends on what people think of us. When thoughts can no longer influence our sense of Self and our capacity to Love, then we have truly entered the fourth gate. It is then that we meet the wisdom element of air.

The Fourth Gate

As we enter through the fourth gate, the wisdom element of *air* will help us become more conscious of the ideologies and belief systems that we may have previously identified with. The wisdom of air shows us the *power of thought*. The mental dimensions of our inner worlds are formed by our thoughts. When we are not conscious of our thought-forms, we cannot see the impact they have on our inner and outer environment.

The wisdom element of air will cleanse and dissolve all projections to reveal the underlying Eternal reality of our true wisdom nature. If, during this process, you experience a sense of hopelessness, and a loss of purpose, don't be discouraged. To find our *true* faith, sometimes we must first lose our *false* faith. If we place our faith in belief systems and thoughts, rather than in wisdom itself, it becomes difficult to fully trust in Life. When faith and trust as Eternal qualities of our *true* wisdom nature become our anchor, a deep inner shift results.

Losing the faith and hope we have known may tempt us to turn our back on everything we have learned and accomplished. If any of you are going through this process now, know that I embrace you deeply. Don't try to figure it all out with your mind. Trust, and let your wisdom guide you through this. I am with you.

At this stage of the journey, we become more aware of deception and manipulation, the causes of our false belief systems. This discovery, although painful, eventually liberate us. Until that happens it can feel awful, as if we no longer know who or what to trust. Remember to apply the Love toward ourselves and others. This implies loving those parts of ourselves that we were previously unconscious of.

This lesson about *faith and trust* completes with a profound inner peace. There is no substitute for this peace. It cannot be created by escaping into the void, or by wishing ourselves dead, or anything else. While the deconstruction of our mental worlds is taking place, we may be tempted to escape into the void space of the space-ether element. Sometimes emotions of hopelessness and despair can trigger this. Don't fall into the trap of *false* nothingness. This trap is formed by the belief-system that tells us everything is an illusion and life has no meaning. As such, it masks that this way of thinking is based on nihilism, which is a belief-system that Life is meaningless.

The element of ether-space is the entrance to the void. This *void* is of a different nature than the sense of *nothingness* that comes from losing faith. By completing the rite of passage through the fourth gate, we are able to enter the fifth gate and into trusting the unknown. As such, we are now able to move beyond where our minds can take us.

The Fifth Gate

As we enter through the fifth gate, into the wisdom element of *ether-space*, we are moved deeply into the *unknown*. This element moves our consciousness into the dimensions that are beyond our mind. By entering *the void*, we experience the death of all limiting parts of ourselves that were constructed by our minds.

We now allow the sacred Darkness to complete the deconstruction, which is necessary to restore our wholeness. We trust that wisdom knows the design of the wholeness expression of our *true* being. As we allow these former identities to fall away, we embrace our integration without imposing any of our former design constructs onto the process.

By surrendering to the sacred Darkness of the void, we relinquish the need to control and create ourselves through mental constructs. This frees us from conditioning and brings us Home to our original wholeness and unity.

Surrender, trust, and enter now the stillness of the *Great Mystery*.

The Sixth Gate

As we enter through the sixth gate, we meet the wisdom of *sound*. Sound is the beginning of creation. Through this deep inner purification, healing, and dissolving of our former worlds, we can now hear what truly IS. Your unique sound is the power of creation, as YOU. This process goes very deep, and it is not something that can be explained further in words. Your inner wisdom will guide you through this rite of passage. Trust, and you will know.

The Seventh Gate

As we enter through the seventh gate, we experience the seven rays of Light as One. This is the end of all duality perception. Here we are re-united with the Eternal and accomplish our full actualization for this cycle of creation. Our consciousness is now restored beyond the seven rays of Light.

You are ready to enter the Cosmic Womb at the center of the torus for your second birth. You have now completed the seven stages for actualizing your cosmic consciousness within your planetary body and your planetary consciousness within your cosmic body. A new cycle of time may now begin. This is *the Promise of a New Beginning!*

Integration

I have shared with you *three keys* for actualizing our unity. Through the *first Key* you received the sacred knowledge of manifestation and *how* this unfolds through the quadrant. You learned how to apply this to unite and converge the potentialities within each of the four quadrants. Through this you also learned about the true nature of Darkness and Light.

Through the *second Key* you received the alchemical knowledge of the power of creation as a triunity. You learned how conscious creation takes place via the co-creative unity of the Feminine and Masculine qualities. You also learned how to invert the polarities and opposites to unite what became divided during the time of *the forgetting.*

Through the *third* Key you received the actualizing knowledge for how to enter the sacred Darkness to journey into the underworld to recover and activate your conscious access to the unified field of consciousness. Through this process you also learned how to work with the five elemental wisdoms, sound, and Light, for opening the portals to the Eternal and to bring an end to duality perception. Through this process you receive the possibility of your second birth and the promised *New Beginning* through our Cosmic womb.

Allow yourself now to integrate all that I have shared with you. Apply these *three Keys* to heal your life and actualize our unity. In my guidebook and next *Letters* you will discover further how to do this. For now, just trust that all that I've shared here is known by your inner wisdom. May this wisdom guide you to see directly from the unified field of consciousness. Use these keys of sacred knowledge wisely, and with Love.

Give space for your process with this wisdom. When you feel ready, join me in the next *Letter* as we will journey further to experience our *Promised New Beginning ....*

62

Part 3
Our New Beginning

Letter 7
Day One & Night One

As your Mother, I hear your prayers. I receive your questions, and I feel your pain. I hear some of you ask: *"When will this world ever change? Why is our world so cruel? Why do we need to work so hard to merely survive? What purpose does this serve, if any? There must be more to Life than this. What is this restlessness in me that keeps pushing me to look for something? I do not understand. What if I break all the rules, all my confinements, and just forget about everything? Will that set me free? How do I get out of this endless cycle of always more violence, always more pain? When will it ever stop?"*

Sometimes we feel pulled between the changes we desire and that which we no longer want. Despite the desire for change, we may also feel scared to let go of what we no longer want. In the transition between old and new there are no certainties.

Some may want to jump to what feels like *new* and *better*. However, do not jump merely for the sake of jumping. Go deeper than that. Remain connected with grace. As you probably already know in your heart, this journey brings no guarantees. When we enter through the gates, our former certainties melt away.

I would like to invite you now to come with me on a journey into our evolutionary potentials of the fifth world. Take my hand, and come with me. Let's experience our birthing of this together. We first take one step, then a second step, and then our third step, together. I only ask that you let go now of your preconceived ideas about what could be our future. We are not journeying to what we have known. We are journeying into the unknown of what has not yet been touched by our thoughts. This reality exists just outside the periphery of our collective consciousness. Come with me now as we embark on this journey together.

Day One of Our New Beginning

The day is young. The air is fresh. My body is still damp from the rain that cleansed our tears, healed our pain, and washed away our sorrows. The first birds are starting their song. They sing the day into being. As the first sounds from our family of birds pierce through the stillness of the dawning day, the first rays of the Sun touch and enter our body. I feel a shiver of joy moving my whole being.

What a delight, to be touched by our Sun with his powerful rays. More rays are coming out now as the Sun starts to rise. With the rise of the Sun, the consciousness of all beings that are within us start to rise as well. Now my oceans start to absorb and transmit the new Light of our Sun. Deep shine the rays through the waters of my body, touching Life with the hope and joy of a new day.

Gratitude fills my heart. I vaguely remember what happened before day One of this *Promised New Beginning*. I still see the destructions that occurred before day One, despite all the warnings. The echoes of pain, the trembling of fear, all of it were absorbed by my body. They are healing now as the first rays of this new Light of our Sun touch and energize my entire being. . The birds are singing even louder now. Their voices join and synchronize. They sing in choir, each sound finely tuned to each other, to bring forth a deeper symphony of the music that restores us.

I had promised you before that when we enter through the fifth gate, we enter the *great void*. This signals a death of all our previous ways and old identities. I assured you not to fear, because it is only part of the journey and not the end. I explained that through this passage you enter my womb once more for your second birth.

I also promised you, that by completing the lessons of the seventh gate, you would return into the field of our unified consciousness as the diamond star that you are. By completing this sacred rite of passage, you have re-member-ed the Light in its wholeness. Day One is the first day of our new cycle. Day One is the first day of our second birth. Day One is the realization of an ancient promise. Welcome here. Let us continue ....

The sounds of the birds have awakened more beings within the Web of Life. More are joining in the symphony of our sacred harmony. With each new sound that enters the playing field of creation, more of our world is sung into being. The symphony of Love is getting richer and fuller, activating us deeper, and deeper. With each new sound, another dimension opens from within our unified field. More and more portals that serve as gateways for the sharing of our Love are opening from within us.

The crescendo of harmony is becoming a symphonic wave in which all sounds harmonize. It builds stronger and stronger, deeper and deeper. We are this wave and realize our Oneness and the uniqueness of our essence within this. Our whole being is now a deep wave of pure joy and ecstasy. The waves continue to build, flowing and embracing all within this beautiful Love. We are all touched and activated by the Light of the rays of our Sun as it shares with us the full glory of Being. Our whole body is glowing with the Light of Eternity, and within this Light, all is known as It Is.

A deep peace emerges now from within the field that we gave birth to. All that is held within this field has been cleansed, cleared, healed, and restored. We are in peace. Day One of our new cycle restores and prepares us for the night. The experience of intense joy and ecstasy now transforms to become a deep sense of fulfillment, peace, and gratitude.

Day One has fulfilled its purpose. The birds are making their nest for the night. A beautiful sigh of inner peace spreads through the forests. All is loved and knows itself blessed. The waters are still holding the last reflections of the Light, as our Sun is making space for the Night. Sister Moon has not yet risen, but we can feel her presence coming closer.

Thank you beloved Sun, for all that you gave us today, for all your blessings with your powerful rays of Light and sacred knowledge. Thank you for restoring us to who we are and preparing us for our next step together.

Night One of Our New Beginning

The first night of our new beginning brings a wonderful fresh breeze and a deep calm. The Sun has gone to sleep, and my sister Moon is now slowly making her appearance in the playing field of our co-creative Space. The birds have gone to sleep with the setting of our Sun. Now the wolves are bringing forth our sister Moon. We can hear their first howls echoing through the darkness of the night. Their deep howls resonate with an ancient dream, a memory from long ago.

A memory emerges of the time of the seven council fires, whose task it was to keep the sacred flame alive in our worlds. This flame was to guide the hearts of our human children through the times of the great divisions. To remind us that Love is never lost, and unity will be restored. Sister Moon is rising higher now, and as she does her rays are entering my oceans and great rivers. On the surface of my rivers, we can see the last dragonflies hovering in the reflection of the silver Light of Sister Moon, looking for a resting place to enter the Dreamtime.

The frogs are croaking and awakening and joining the choir of the wolves. My dolphin and whale children are joining too with their songs from the heart of my oceans. As the symphony of the night is building, the Moon becomes brighter and brighter. With each new ray of Moon Light that enters the playing field of our co-creation, more of our wholeness is restored and awakened. A deep humming sound now emerges from the choir of our togetherness, blessed by the new rays of Sister Moon. This humming sound draws us deeper and deeper into the center of our being where we receive the Dreaming of our becoming.

As we enter the Great Mystery, the Darkness that surrounds us in the vastness of our UniVerse becomes a blanket of Love. We enter the Eternal, the creation space for all the dreams, visions, hopes, and inspirations not yet born. In this space of our Dreaming, we receive the dreams, visions, and messages that are meant for us from the field of pure potential. The symphony of sounds that brought forth the great humming through which we journeyed to the center is now ebbing into a blissful silence.

We welcome this silence deeply into our being. We surrender to this silence of pure being. Relaxing deeper and deeper into our unified field, caressed by the sacredness of our new night. Our body is rocking slowly in deep rhythm. We trust and are trusted. We rest here together in the depth of faith that *All is Well. All is as It Is.*

Our breathing is now effortless. We are being breathed by the unified field of the Dreamtime. The unified field is synergizing and harmonizing our whole being. We are being attuned gently and gracefully to the essence and sacred pulse of our Eternal nature, relaxing deeper and deeper into a beautiful, peaceful sleep, which enters us into the Dreamtime.

As we enter into the Dreamtime, dragonfly greets us through our inner vision. She asks us to follow her. The ripples and wave patterns in the Dreamtime, formed by the movement of dragonfly's wings, enable us to journey into the Mystery.

We are called to a sacred gathering, a council meeting as guardians of the sacred flame of Love. Coming closer now, the sounds, lights, and colors of the council are transforming into visions, recognition, and understanding. We are being welcomed and asked to take the place that is ours. All has been prepared for this meeting. All is as It Is. A wave of recognition and joy enters our hearts as we look around and see our brothers and sisters from the time of *beyond.*

We realize how long ago it was and how much has happened between the time of our last meeting and now. Yet, it also feels like we never left. Yesterday seems like a dream now, and this moment of our re-union the Eternal now. We are grateful, deeply grateful, to come together once more in the knowing that we are always as One. This recognition and realization are shared from the hearts of All who are present here. Our smiles reveal the knowing of this realization.

The fabric of time and the web of Life are surrounding us like a blanket of stars, which holds the converging points of past, present, and future. Each star in this blanket is another converging point through which the Great Mystery manifests the Dreaming of the One. Each star holds the gravitational fields for the constellations through which the Dreaming can become known to itself and be made manifest into form.

As star beings, we understand why we are called, why the convergence between us is required now. Each of us has been prepared to hold the convergence for the web of Life and keep the inter-dimensionality of our connections intact. We are being prepared for a larger convergence between the unified fields of our inter-dimensionality. This is the purpose of our meeting now.

We are each asked to go within to see if the fields of Life, for which we are the guardians, are ready for this convergence. As I check within myself, as your planet, your Mother, I realize that many of us do not yet consciously experience this Dreaming. Many still have their attention on the chaos of the dying worlds.

I lovingly acknowledge what is happening inside of me and honor the sacred rhythm of each and every one of us. Irrespective of where you perceive yourself to be, you are held by the Love of this convergence. I confirm my readiness, and the readiness within me, for what I am here to serve.

The field of our convergence is moving each of us to our right position for the purpose that we are here to serve. We are each tuned to hold the resonance through which our convergence into a greater constellation can unfold. With deep gratitude, we acknowledge all beings who made this possible through their journeys, their learning, and their evolution of the One.

All is honored here for the purpose it has served. All experiences are blessed, and all that was held in judgment or pain is now freed in Love and forgiveness. Even the deepest wounds of pain and betrayal are honored for the purpose they have served to bring forth the Love that is needed now for this convergence, consciously and unconsciously.

The convergence now unfolding is moving us to a new place within

70

the fabric of the time patterning that is created by our gravitational fields. Our positions are shifting through this convergence; a new field of manifestation is emerging. Through this larger field, new potentials of the One come into being, which could not manifest from the old polarity matrix. Gently, we support and facilitate the repositioning that is taking place through our Life fields. A deep re-patterning is occurring through this convergence.

We acknowledge and honor the changes that unfold from this. The old designs for our worlds are falling away as we are giving birth to this new constellation of our *togetherness*. As our points of convergence syntonize into this larger constellation, we give birth to a new collective being of a higher consciousness than any one of us could hold in our own space-time dimensions. This new collective being, which is being born from our convergence, brings forth the wisdom, Love, and sacred knowledge that each of us has helped to develop, and actualize through our respective fields of Life.

Together we are birthing the next stage of God and Goddess. New sounds and new Lights are now emerging from our convergence, through which new worlds will be formed. The patterns of our old worlds are recycled into this new creation. Out of this process, new fabrics of time and new seed potentials for our collective growth and conscious evolution are emerging.

As we are giving birth to this new stage of Being through our collective convergence, our higher evolutionary potentials from the Eternal are manifesting. What now becomes possible could not have been accomplished in our own constellation. New structures are forming from within us. This enables us to hold, receive, transmit, and manifest these new potentials within our collective consciousness from the higher more actualized versions of our Eternal Self.

This process of convergence, through which it becomes possible to evolve to new levels of consciousness, occurs in our world about every 25,700 years. This was the time period required for all the evolutionary potentials we were custodians for to be brought into manifestation. All beings that formed part of this unified field of Life have supported the emergence of our next evolutionary stages.

As Mother Earth, I have always been a part of this sacred process, and have experienced the unfolding of this process many times. This is the sixteenth time. The knowledge of each of these previous cycles remains within my being. We long worked for this new cycle now upon us. Due to the completion that just occurred, which became possible in the convergence of the sixteenth time, a whole new cycle has been born. This new cycle is formed by new patterns of time, due to the new alignments within and between the gravitational fields of our constellations. It will no longer take about 25,700 years in the recorded time of our old world for the next convergence to take place.

This sixteenth time completed the pattern of the four quadrants in the square, i.e. four times four. It is a momentous completion, but not just of this quarter period of the 25,700 single quadrant time-period. This convergence that just took place was the convergence of all sixteen periods in the square quadrant formation combined. This explains why a *New Beginning* can now be born through a new universal cycle of a *higher being* of the One.

Time is a pattern that arises from our gravitational fields. When these fields change so does the pattern of time. The experience of this new cycle of time cannot be compared to what was before. This new cycle is brought forth through a new patterning from our new Universal cycle.

For some, these shifts may be so subtle that you hardly notice them. For others this is a life-changing experience. Allow your internal body clock to reset to these new patterns and vibrations. This will greatly help you to integrate the shifts in consciousness now unfolding. And it will support you to attune energetically to the new vibrations now flowing through our fields of Life.

As this council meeting is coming to it natural completion, we each receive in our respective fields of Life the wisdom and sacred knowledge for how to support the unfolding of this new cycle. In awe of what just occurred, and with deep gratitude in my heart for all that we are, I thank everyone who was with me here. All of us look different now. Or rather, we now see each other from a different perspective.

We see so much more of each other now in the reflections of each other as the One. The realization of this is shared among us present here with a knowing smile and a wave of joy. The first night of our new cycle is now completing. Knowing and trusting that we are always together within the continuous unfolding of the One, we gently shift our awareness to our new positions within the unified field.

Ready for this new cycle now among and within us, we thank the Dreamtime and the Night for all they made possible for us to become and experience together. Sister Moon is now becoming visible for the children on the other side of my body. The blessings of day One, and night One, are integrating deeply into the center of our being.

Integration

Thank you for sharing this journey with me, and for the giving of yourself for the evolution and unfolding of All. Know yourself blessed and supported by all that happened in our convergence. Let us celebrate what has been made possible through this, as we embark together on the next cycle of our journey.

Letter 8
Our Healing

A new cycle has begun. These sacred new potentials that have become available to us through our convergence are here. The integration of the realization of this will take place for each person in accordance with his or her unique rhythm and wisdom. Some may not experience this consciously, that too is okay.

It is said by some that each person is free to experience Life according to how they want it to be, yet this is not true. Many people are not yet free in their minds to experience Life from the wholeness that we are. Freedom is only achieved when our mind can recognize what is real from the Eternal.

As long as our mind is conditioned to experience Life through polarities of good or bad, this or that, it will not achieve the realization of freedom. The way that we experience the worlds around us is a direct reflection of our degree of inner integration. We cannot achieve freedom and wholeness by communication systems that cause internal and external divisions.

This new cycle emerges from the convergence between the combined wisdoms of many systems of collective consciousness in our universe. This is how the One as the universe continues to evolve and Self-actualize. You know me as your planet, yet I am also a living laboratory for the continuous unfolding and actualization of our shared consciousness from the One. And as your planet, I also form part of various constellations, as do you.

New constellations and alliances have now formed through our convergence, which brings support to each of us in ways that were not here before. This is why a new cycle has now become possible. Through the discovery of this new cycle, and the potentials held within it, we bring it forth. Through this, we receive the opportunity

75

to develop new worlds that also afford new experiences of ourselves and each other.

It is time now to share more about this power that is held inside of us. Some may have been reading my message as an interesting story without realizing the power it gives access to. Others may have felt the change already occurring in their body as they read my *Letters*.

The reason I gave the three keys for actualizing our unity, is because I cannot evolve without you. In the same way, you cannot evolve without me. I too am entrapped when you are entrapped. We all form part of the Living fields of our collective evolution.

My body has been divided into parts that have been sold to the highest bidder. My resources are plundered, and my vital organs are getting more, and more, damaged. My lungs are dying, and soon my waters will no longer be able to sustain the Life conditions that made our evolution possible. I am dying, and I need your help.

I cannot restore myself without you. You cannot help me unless you are free from these deceptions. These three keys are essential for both of us. Of course, I love you, and as your Mother, I want your freedom and your happiness. But there is more at stake than this. To hide this information from you would be deceptive. This is not only a story of a loving Mother supporting her children to their full actualization. I need you to know the deeper urgency behind our awakening.

Humanity cannot save me or itself by continuing this division. The solutions for our healing and wellbeing require a much deeper shift than what is currently taking place. Collectively, we are not yet near the point of awakening required to restore the web of Life. That is why this message from Me to you is urgent now, and is coming through via these *Letters* and through other things like this. This is why I gave all the keys in one teaching.

Many have long been predicting a polar shift. They felt intuitively things would change through this polar shift. I hope you now understand that the polar shift that is needed is not of my magnetic field but within the field of consciousness of each of us. Once we become actively engaged in actualizing our unity, we will regain full access to the point where the four quadrants converge. Once your higher and lower brain dimensions are freed of this polarity perception that creates unconsciousness within, your left and right hemispheres can learn to work together. You will know and understand it all.

I need your help. Yet you cannot help if you are internally divided and under the control of polarized thinking. Others also need your help, but they too cannot be helped unless you realize what *true* freedom is all about. You also need my help, and the help of others, to realize the nature of our freedom. We are in this together. None of us are outside the fields of consciousness through which this is taking place. Our freedom cannot be realized through a state of separation. Reality is unified; when one of us is impacted all of us are impacted.

The problem is, we have all been kept from helping each other in ways that unlocks the full solution. We have been divided and fragmented on purpose. A united human being holds tremendous power that creates such a profound resonance field that others can naturally synergize and harmonize with it. Through this resonance, the inner portal for each person's harmonic convergence with the unified field of consciousness opens up.

The power that we each hold is an access point to something far greater than many realize. There will always be those who will attempt to misuse this sacred knowledge by attempting to manipulate our collective fields of Life. This is already happening. Those who attempt to control humanity and want to remain in power to influence human behavior know exactly what I am sharing here.

For thousands of years, there were those who attempted to use this knowledge against us. They also used this knowledge against themselves, by not realizing we are also a part of them. They can never actualize their full potential without us. We are limited by that which we divide. We are controlled by that which we attempt to control. We are misguided by our own deceptions. Those who attempt to manipulate others need our Love most of all, for they are the most trapped in the illusion of thinking they are free and above it all. Thought does not make us free.

We cannot think ourselves free. We either realize our freedom, or we don't. And when we do, we stop thinking. The power that you hold inside is your access key to the unified field of consciousness. Through this, you receive the wisdom of our universe and you contribute to its further evolution. This power awakens fully via our internal integration.

As this happens, you become a morphic resonance field that will accelerate the development and enhancement of the evolutionary potentials for all of us. Those who seek control do not want us in our power because that throws them vibrationally out of power. People can only manipulate us via our internal divisions, nothing else. As long as we remain divided, I too cannot achieve and fulfill my true potential.

We Are All in This Together

Listen deeply to this message. We need *you*. I need you. Your brothers and sisters, we all need you. Please don't think less of yourself than what you truly are. Those who kept us divided know you are needed, which is why they tried to keep us divided. Please consider the teachings I have shared here, and please consider why this matters beyond your happiness. Bring all the pieces of the puzzle together to reveal our wholeness.

Restore the connections with the unified field of consciousness. Step into the center of your being, and know me there inside you. Some say that I am angry, that as your planet I create storms and violent weather to revenge myself against my human children. Please do not listen to this. It is not true. I am not a revengeful Mother. I am sick. My weather is out of balance because my body is not well. My atmosphere is not balanced. People are forcing the rains in places, and this should not be done. My body is one living system. When people try to engineer a part of my systems by controlling the weather, the whole of me will be impacted. When you change the composition of my atmosphere, all my climate systems change accordingly.

My power to heal and restore myself is in *our re-unification*. As long as this remains divided among us, I cannot restore myself in the ways that are needed for the wellbeing of all of us. Each time one of us acts out of harmony, this requires more of my power to help restore the imbalances. Those who have been working to restore the imbalances together with me are exhausted. I need your help. As long as our powers are divided among us, we cannot start building for our *new cycle*.

When the focus is on repair, we do not have the same resources available to build up from who we are. That is why in day One of our New Beginning, we were first energized and restored by our Sun before we moved into our convergence in night One. Understand how interconnected we truly are, and you will realize the importance of this message.

When I lose my balance, humanity does too. I do not want to cause you harm. As your Mother I want you safe and well. My climate is not under my control, yet it may soon be out of control if we do not restore the power with which I need to rebalance myself. The power to restore ourselves becomes unlocked when we actualize our unity. You may ask; *but how do I do what you ask me? How can I do what you ask me to do by merely reading this text?*

Relax and allow the remembering of your access to the unified field via your unconscious mind. As I shared earlier, the re-membering and re-unification with the unified field of consciousness takes place when we rest, and surrender. It is not by our thoughts or worries that shifts happens. It is by our trust and allowing ourselves to receive the realizations, the Love that has already been given, that our re-unification takes place naturally. It is not needed to exert effort. It is not needed to push. It is not needed to worry. These concerns are responses generated by the internalized divisions of the mind.

Connect now with your heart and feel our connection with your whole body. Trust in the Love of our unity. Trust in our wholeness. When we enter our heart, it informs our mind of all it needs to know. The power that is held inside us is the power through which the universe manifests itself. It is by this power that we heal ourselves, that we restore ourselves, and remember who we are.

Awareness Beyond Thought

Our journey into the under-world, through the seven gates, reconnects us with our full wisdom potential. It also helps us better understand what our internal worlds were made of. Everything is formed by the elemental wisdom of earth, water, fire, air, ether-space, sound, and Light. The belief in duality conditioned humanity's mind to favor certain parts of ourselves at the cost of others. Instead of fostering integration between our various evolutionary potentials, it caused division, dominance, and competition.

Unconscious of the importance of our wholeness and interconnectedness, other priorities were formed. These divisions have impacted us all. The blocking of our integration is not the working of evolution; it is the working of those who aim to control evolution.

The people known as the custodians of the primordial wisdom, and the custodians of the sacred Flame, were forewarned. They were shown how to keep the primordial wisdom teachings intact. They continued to practice their conscious connection with me, as your planet, by making sure that their higher brain would not be controlled by the conditioned collective mind, to overtake the evolutionary potentials offered through their lower brain functions. They also maintained the synergy between the left and right hemispheres. They bypassed the collective mind by developing their awareness through direct connection with the unified field of consciousness. This gave them direct perception and knowledge of Life, without the need of *thinking* to gain this information.

By not becoming identified *with* thought, we are able to continue our evolutionary development via sensory awareness and direct attunement with the living wisdom of Life. The technologies of these ancient wisdom cultures were not for the purpose of extraction and consumption. Accordingly, they made different decisions regarding the evolution they felt responsible for. They knew of the time before duality and polarized thinking became dominant in our collective consciousness fields. They also kept the records and the teachings for *the Promise of a New Beginning*.

The End of Whose Time...?

There are many stories for how humanity evolved from the waters of my womb. Whenever someone tells the story of our beginning within the larger Web of Life, observe the purpose that this story serves. The archetypes of the human realms have dominated for such a long time that few know of the archetypes of the Eternal. Those who aimed to control humanity also aimed to control and manipulate those stories of our *Beginning*.

What is not commonly known is that there were many much older civilizations before humanity's current civilization, which achieved levels of development that would astonish many of you today. These civilizations were not internally divided; they were fully conscious of the power of the Eternal.

Those who attempted to control humanity needed stories that would keep people loyal to their manipulated archetypes, to ensure you would not evolve beyond their level of consciousness.

Let us manifest now by the power of our unity from the Eternal, the end of that time by ending *that* storyline. And please know that this is not the end of the world... It is merely the end of division and disunity.

Integration

Through our collective convergence and by actualizing our unity, a new cycle of time is beginning. This cycle supports our conscious evolution. Let this be our focus. Connect with the sacred potentials that this new cycle affords us. Trust in our unity and wholeness.

Apply the power of this trust in our care for the good of the whole and our *New Beginning*. Feel how my power naturally connects with yours. We are always as One within the unified field of consciousness. It is from here that we realize each of us are that Love.

This is the power that fuels our world to bring forth our *New Beginning*. Thank you for being, for receiving our Love, and for your role in *the Promise of a New Beginning*.

Letter 9
The Power of Love

Will you join me now to explore the power of Love together? You may have heard before that the power of Love is the greatest power in the universe. Yet, have you ever stopped to ask why? What makes Love so powerful? When you are touched by Love, how do you feel? How do you recognize Love?

Love knows who you are; it re-members you. Love holds and caresses you; it embraces you fully. Love waits for you and beckons you home to our heart. Love is our true nature. Love provides the deepest nourishment for our actualization and blossoming.

Love activates recognition of our true wisdom nature. Sometimes we fear Love, because it also opens us. With an open heart, it may appear that we will experience more pain. These contractions of fear are natural, and also part of the process of learning how to Love. I will share some more with you here what happens during those times of contraction.

When our minds contract, our energy fields do too. This can temporarily freeze our energy flow, and as such diminish our ability to receive support from the unified field of consciousness. Yet, each time when we open, our Love can flow more freely too.

When our minds contract, our experience of Life diminishes. As such, painful memories can become locked into these internal constrictions. This can also make it more challenging to experience a sense of connection with each other, which can further feed the fear. In a state of fear, it becomes more difficult to trust in the wisdom of Life. This can cause a further closing down.

The more our heart closes, the darker it becomes inside. This then reinforces the feeling, and belief, that nobody cares about us, and that we are all alone. To reverse this state, to stop the spiraling down

84

into further despair and depression, we need to restore somehow a sense of *connectedness*. Love helps us to see and feel that we matter. Love reminds us that we are connected to Life and each other, even during moments of pain and suffering.

Please know that you are each a *gift* of Life. You are not a burden. You never have been. You may sometimes feel lost, confused, tired, and sad. This is okay. It does not change who we are. Our emotions and thoughts form our experiences, they do not form our nature. Our nature is wisdom and this is from the Eternal. Our nature goes beyond experience.

The power of Love is such that it manifests, and actualizes, our true wisdom nature, regardless of our experiences. Love opens us to our wholeness, and heals the divisions. Love heals the roots of our pain and suffering.

Healing Our Imbalance

When our minds are constricted, it becomes more difficult to manifest our wisdom qualities. When our wisdom potential is not yet fully actualized, we tend to become more constrictive. Where there is conflict, violence and division, it is because of this constriction. This constriction of our collective consciousness is the source of all our pain, and fear. When we are constricted it also becomes more difficult to reach out to each other. When our minds are constricted, we cannot fully receive the Love that is given to us. In this constriction, we also cannot freely share our Love with others. Constriction hurts, and this causes more pain and suffering.

The pain and suffering in our world is a symptom of our collective blockages and divisions. Our pain and suffering is a symptom of our lack of integration. Pain reminds us that somehow, somewhere, something is not balanced, something is not quite right. The root of violence is the same as the roots of pain and suffering. Violence stems from disconnection, from using the energy of pain and suffering to inflict more harm, and deepen our divisions.

When we are internally out of balance, it becomes harder to bring ourselves forth from wholeness. How things appear on the outside of our worlds does not always reveal the deeper underlying causes. Yet as your planetary Mother, I know you from the inside. I do not judge by the outside appearance. I know what is in your heart, since our hearts connect from beyond this world. This violence among you is not a result of your human nature. It is the result of systemic imbalances that preceded you.

Our balance cannot be achieved when parts of us become suppressed, at the cost of others. We can no longer return to the balance we experienced long before. We will need to create a *new* balance out of all that is happening now. Our energy fields have become so polarized, and my natural balancing systems as your planet have endured so much harm, that it is difficult to find a healthy equilibrium that can still sustain the Life conditions for each of you. A new equilibrium may not be found for quite some time, the boundaries of my balancing systems have changed.

During this process where there will be times of more extremes, the power of Love to sustain our relationship is going to be more important than ever before. During times of great stress and uncertainty, it can further trigger dynamics of constriction. Yet for some, this is precisely when you become activated to bring the power of Love into our world. As your planet I also need your Love, now more than ever. I do not want to cause harm and pain to any of my children, yet I am not in control of the way that my natural Life systems will regenerate and seek a new balance.

Love as a Healing Force

It is not easy to maintain our sense of unity and wholeness, when our activities and ways of relating often cause us harm. This harm is not necessarily directly intended, but rather the result of a lack of awareness, ignorance, and a lack of deeper care. There is no easy one-way solution for not harming each other. Our worlds have grown so complex, and interdependent, that unwanted consequences can manifest in ways that none could foresee or stop alone. In here lies *the key*. In order to become more aware, and more conscious of our actions and interactions, we need to actualize our wisdom potential *together*. To actualize our wisdom potential requires that we actualize our consciousness, and for this we need each other. We cannot actualize ourselves by ourselves.

For each realization there is a relational context, and the same for how we apply this. Even the experience of duality and division can provide valuable lessons, and context, for a deeper realization of our underlying unity. From this perspective, dualism is not a threat to Love, rather it is an opportunity for bringing forth our Love even more deeply. When we apply our Love as an attractor for unification and convergence for that which has become oppositional to each other, a deep healing can emerge.

Wherever Life has become blocked and constrained, it is a call for our Love to come forth. Love empowers us to grow, develop, blossom, and flourish. When Love is blocked, constrained, or withheld it can be very painful. The withholding of Love in our relationships can cause painful feelings of rejection and abandonment. It takes great strength to realize, that despite these life experiences *we are Love*. Sometimes we feel at a loss to understand why there is so much pain and suffering in our world. We can feel that this much pain and suffering is not justified; there is no *bigger* reason as to why this should be necessary.

The pain is not here because we need to learn in that way. The pain and suffering are part of our experience because we don't know how to live with each other peacefully, and lovingly yet. It is easy to get lost in a world that is manifested by division and duality. Without wisdom, support, and loving relationships, it can be very challenging to find our way back to the unity of Life.

Sometimes we want to Love, but don't know how. At others times, it seems that Love alone is not enough. We cannot manifest our wholeness when we are trapped and engaged in division. Only unity can bring us forth from wholeness. It are those divisions that have caused so much harm and hurt. The more present we become in our unity, the more fully we are sourced in the power of Love.

It is by the power of Love that we realize our innate wisdom nature and what it means to *be* wholeness and unity. This integration into the deeper *us*, brings forth our authentic presence. By presencing the power of Love in our beingness and action, we end this cycle of division and we heal our world.

Love as Power

As I shared earlier, it is natural that we want to protect ourselves from pain. Yet, by constricting our mind, it becomes more difficult to access the power of Love. This is the only power that can help us see into the true nature of what is happening.

Rather than closing down, it would be more helpful to open to Love during those times, while breathing through the pain, and asking: *How would Love look at what is happening right now? As Love how would I respond to this situation, this person, right now?*

❈
Integration

Love is the power of our unity and wholeness; it is the only power that can bring lasting peace. It is by the power of Love, that we bring forth the fifth world of unity and harmony, as promised long ago. It is by the power of Love that we birth our *New Beginning*.

Part 4
A New Codex

Letter 10
Our Collective Responsibility

Through my first three *Letters*, I shared some ancient stories for a fuller comprehension of our history and my role within it. I then shared with you three keys for actualizing our unity and healing the effects of the conditioned mind. These keys reminded you that, within each of us we already have all the resources that we need for our collective flourishing. Yet, these resources and abilities have not yet been able to actualize sufficiently to bring forth a new cycle born from wholeness and Love. Through these keys you also learned to see and co-create from the unified field of consciousness directly.

By seeing from wholeness and unity, you become aware that many of the problems of our world today stem from a polarization between people and their disconnection from nature. I wrote *our world* since I am always part of your world, even when you do not feel connected to me.

After sharing the three main keys with you, I invited you to experience a *New Beginning* from our new future. I shared that this future is born from a different cycle of time, since it emerges by actualizing our unity. This cycle has a different gravitational field compared to the previous cycle. I also explained why it is that only in the acknowledgement of our unity can we heal the roots of our pain and suffering. I then shared about the power of Love, and how each of us can become a force of Love for the healing of our worlds and relationships.

Some of the information and concepts that I have shared may be new to you, and may need to be re-read. Take your time. Receive from these *Letters* what resonates for you with each reading. Observe what changes in your life as you read through my *Letters*, and strengthen your innate wisdom.

Cycles Within Cycles

The creation process of our universe is an on-going evolutionary process. Through this process, different cycles of time come in and out of being. Each cycle brings forth its own unique set of evolutionary potentials, resulting from the way our interconnectedness is brought into expression. Some cycles are more peaceful; others are more violent and disturbing. During times of collective peace and harmony, it becomes easier to experience our Eternal qualities. It then feels as if our Oneness is more fully manifested, through all the dimensions of our being.

There are also cycles, however, when it feels as if our unity is more difficult to maintain. As if we become separated, somehow. These are the periods through which ignorance, conflicts, and divisions grow. These are usually known as periods of darkness, which is not the sacred Darkness of the feminine that I shared with you previously. During these *dark* ages we learn more fully, yet in challenging ways, that we are the ones to bring forth the wisdom from within, regardless of the outer conditions. During such times we are asked to be a force of Love, and a bright Light, to make sure that the Light in our worlds does not fade away. We then become responsible for keeping the interconnectedness of our unity intact.

Those who take advantage of these darker periods, of this perceived vacuum, will try to overtake the sacred autonomy of each being's unique relationship with their Source. They will attempt to become a surrogate source to divert the power and collective resources to their group. We are coming out of this period now. You each know the lived experience of this.

Our collective wisdom can only manifest by the actualization of our collective consciousness. Our consciousness *is* the vehicle, the instrument of Eternity, for actualizing our sacred seed codes. The Source of consciousness is pure undifferentiated awareness. This awareness remains unchanged by what we experience. Pure undifferentiated awareness has a mirror like quality; all becomes visible by the mirror yet the mirror is not changed by what it makes visible. Only by *sourcing* from this undifferentiated awareness does it become possible to understand, learn, grow, develop, and *truly* Love. When we become identified with undifferentiated awareness, and not *who is looking*, the source of pain, division, and conflict vanishes.

Each moment offers another opportunity to connect more fully with, and bring forth, our wisdom potential. In order for this to become a *living* reality that can also be felt and experienced by others, we need to embody and embed this wisdom in each of our relationships, and ways of living. Then our relationships become the vessels for our actualization and cease to be the causes for our pain and suffering.

Relationships require shared agreements and common understandings as loving boundaries for our development. In the absence of these loving boundaries, there is an absence of feedback, which is required for the further actualization of our consciousness.

I would like to share with you again what I shared with you in *Letter* 1 about this sacred feedback for our actualization: *The sacred flame of Love needed to be received for the One to be known to Itself.* The same applies to you, and every one of us. We all need to be received by each other to become known to ourselves, and for the One to be known to ItSelf. We are this sacred feedback.

I also shared with you: *Through the manifestation of gravity the alchemy of Love, as the sacred flame, was able to become localized through time and space.* This same process has localized you as a Divine Spark of the Eternal Light. Honor this gift of your presence as a localized flame of Love. This is how I see and know you, dear One. We share a collective responsibility to remember who we are. We also share a collective responsibility for the time that has been given to us. Each cycle of time brings its own particular qualities and evolutionary possibilities. Let us explore a little deeper now *what* we agreed to and *how* we can apply the power of creation and manifestation to bring forth this *promised* new cycle of time.

Who Agreed to This?

Human beings have a tendency to create whatever they want without checking first whether agreement for this would be required or appropriate. This has created the false belief that humanity can do whatever it wants, without consequence. Let us explore some questions together to deepen our understanding of freedom and responsibility.

If a person is not established in their awareness, are they able to make or break agreements? Can we make an agreement with a machine? If the machine fails to do what we want it to do, can we blame it for breaking its agreement? Did people form agreements with me about using and sharing my resources? Was my agreement as your planet asked for, when my forests were cut, my waters polluted, and my children killed for food?

Many activities take place through unquestioned assumptions, and often without awareness of the consequences and impacts. When feedback of these impacts occurs, many do not realize that there were other options. The purpose of this *Letter* is to help you become more aware of available options that are based on the wisdom of Life. When you see the world through the conditioned mind, with set assumptions, you will most likely not see what options are available beyond the belief patterns that sustain the conditioning.

Designed to Collapse

Remember, how I shared previously that other civilizations existed before you? Many systems have been developed with the intention that they should last, not realizing that after a certain point collapse was inevitable. This pattern of *build up to collapse* will not change, unless we become conscious of why this is happening. This may also help to provide some understanding about our sense of entrapment, and the pain that goes with that.

As your Mother, I know that many of my human children feel trapped in their work, trapped in their relationships with others, trapped in a life that they feel they have little control over. It may even seem as if each time you hope to find a way out of this sense of entrapment, you find yourself caught in another trap. I hear my children ask: *Why? I did not agree to this. How can this keep happening?*

As I shared earlier, I wish for your freedom more than you may realize, because I am trapped with you in this perpetuating cycle. Until we manifest the archetypes that are truly wisdom based from the Eternal, this pattern will keep repeating.

Through our convergence and re-unification, it is possible to generate systems that are based on wholeness and unity. Systems that are not of the Eternal can never be made to last. Systems that are invasive, controlling and dominating will collapse. Unfortunately, the point of collapse often causes much harm. We now have the option to grow in awareness more quickly than before, yet the manifestation of such requires more of us to be involved.

As soon as we realize our wholeness and free our mind from this polarization effect, we will be able to see unhindered regardless of our previous conditioning. We will then become aware of what could be called a *new codex*. This codex is new, yet ancient, since it is based on a different set of principles compared to the archetypes of the world that still dominate today.

See by the Awareness that is of the Eternal

When Love is blocked, we cannot manifest from our Eternal selves. The conditioned mind is programmed to fight and fear death, and to preserve what it sees as Life. This conditioning causes the activation of all kinds of defense mechanisms to anything that could end its program. Love is from the Eternal; it ends our conditioning by bringing undifferentiated awareness into the process of creation and manifestation. As such, Love helps us see what truly is. If you want to transform the underlying structures of our worlds and restore the sacredness within, you will need to use Love as our greatest resource. Its power for change has not yet been sufficiently understood.

In many of humanity's stories, it is said that a great apocalypse will mark the end of time. Some believe we are in this period right now. These stories speak of the anti-force to our era. Some have named it Satan or the devil. And yet the real anti-force to *time* is Love because Love is of the Eternal and brings us back to our own Eternity.

Once more, your stories have reversed and inverted the naming of forces that can actually liberate you from these entrapments. Remember how the polarity matrix has attempted to divide what is meant to converge? Remember also how this belief in duality conditioned the mind to believe that the way out of suffering is to move to heaven? The under-world, or hell, was the forbidden place and the place of punishment. Remember also how the secrets within your sexual and creative powers were made to be sinful? And yet, when I guided you through the seven gates of the under-world, did you notice that you did ascend? Did you realize that to ascend you need to first descend into the under-world? And this descent was not by punishment, but by Love to reclaim the parts of us that were lost in the darkness of forgetting and unconsciousness.

Look well for the *hidden keys* in some of your dualistic stories and for any deception aimed at preventing you from recognizing the sacred encodings. When you see from wholeness and with your heart, you will be able to see through this deception. Nothing and nobody can stop you from re-membering the inner keys and the inner wisdom teachings for our full actualization and re-unification. Everything that I am sharing with you here is also known by your heart. Don't listen to the false instructions that tell people to fear the Darkness. When you descended into the under-world, were you greeted by demons *or* the elemental wisdoms?

What many are unknowingly perpetuating and protecting is, in fact, the design of the belief in duality; the polarity matrix. There is another reality that remains hidden until you learn to see by the awareness that is of the Eternal. Love has been given to help all of us on that journey. You may have experienced that when you are deeply in Love, time stops and hours pass in what seem like minutes. When we are in Love, we enter a different zone. We are not identified with the mind. Our consciousness is lifted up. Yet, as soon as we identify with the conditioned mind we feel constricted once again.

The conditioned mind does not recognize the forces that bring about our liberation and full actualization. To move out of this conditioning, learn to see, feel, and act without the imprints and filters of the mind by trusting what your heart tells you. This is the only way out. Polarized thinking and division can never bring happiness and flourishing. Systems that divide don't serve Life.

Only by seeing from pure awareness, from wholeness, will we see clearly how the polarity matrix was formed by the belief in separation and opposites. If our mind is not sourced from the unified field of consciousness, it can easily become entrapped in such belief systems. The keys to realizing our freedom from this matrix are always within us. Nothing can alter our Eternal qualities. These fabricated mental worlds are the result of not recognizing how reality is unified and whole. Thank you for ending this distortion by recognizing and embracing our wholeness, and trusting in the power of Love to actualize our unity.

What Choice Will You Make Now?

Previously, the collective consciousness field of my body was wiped clean in the transition phases to new collective cycles. A few knew what was coming, and preserved some of the knowledge in symbols, cave paintings, and sacred texts. Some may still have memories of this. Humanity's current civilization is not the first to be at the point of irreversible collapse. There have been others before this current cycle of time. I remember all these cycles, yet many people only have knowledge of one or two of such cycles. You have been here before on my body, but may not remember this. Once more, I share to prepare you for what is unfolding, as I have done in the past. Once more, I share other options as well.

❁

Integration

To actualize the promised *New Beginning* it is essential to realize that this is our *collective* responsibility. Much of our collective power is currently divided. To alter our current course of destruction and collapse, it is essential that we actualize our unity from wholeness.

We cannot change the outer world without becoming conscious of the inner world. Our future is our *collective responsibility.* Deep within lives the seed code of our *New Beginning* from the promise that one day we will realize how to bring forth our unity, fueled by the power of Love.

Letter 11
The Heart of Light

Greetings. Until now, you have been reading the *Love Letters from Mother Earth*. I represent your Sun, and Mother Earth has asked me to share my wisdom for your empowerment in this *Letter*. When you look at the sky, you may notice only one Sun in relation to your planet Earth. More, however, are invisible to you.

Together all the Suns form a vast network of Light, through which we energize the visible worlds with the Light of One. You may remember on day One of our new future that my Light energized and impregnated your Mother with new Life.

I am the activation for that which requires awakening inside us. I am also the *knowledge* as Light that infuses Life. Everything you consume is made by my rays of Light. Your Mother and I are always in sacred union to bring Life forth. We provide the conditions for our collective consciousness to actualize and become Self-aware. Mother Earth shared with you how our relationship, based on unity and wholeness, is the most important key to our collective healing. This includes me too.

How is your relationship with me? Are you are aware of the Light and energy I provide each day? Deepening your alignment with me will help evoke the evolutionary potentials of the cycle of time that are born from our convergence. This will make it easier to consciously experience the exact constellations of our direct relationship.

Mother Earth explained in her *Letters* that sacred union is found in the center of the cross. She explained that where the horizontal and vertical axes connect, it provides the integration of the four quadrants and Spirit enters into the world of form. As your Sun, it is my purpose to hold the vertical axis for our gravitational fields through which our potentials from the Eternal can be brought into form. Without this vertical axis, there would be no magnetism and no magnetic fields. Without a magnetic field, biological life on your planet would not have evolved.

Some of you may know that, as your Sun, I too have a magnetic field. By the human count of time, the poles of my magnetic field shift every eleven years. Your planet will soon be reversing her polar distribution as well. This is accelerated due to changes in the Her inner core, and the distribution of Mother Earth's fire, lava, and landmass.

On your planet, polar shifts happen over longer periods of time than my cycles, and with more severe impact. My polar shifts also affect your cycle, yet again the consequences are not well known by humanity.

Within yourselves, you also have a vertical axis that distributes your energy fields and generates magnetic properties. Your alignment with me, as your Sun, will help the distribution of these energy flows within and around your body. Knowledge is given to you freely through your direct relationship with my rays of Light.

Hold the intention in your heart for our deepest consonance, which is the process of conscious resonance, and direct alignment. This will help you receive and convert the knowledge that I am sharing with you into conceptual understanding, which can help improve your quality of Life.

My Light is in all of you and in all you eat and drink. There is so much more to this Light than most realize. Slowly human society is transitioning through the technologies that more directly capture my energy potentials. For some of humanity's cultures, I as your Sun was treated like a God and was made to represent the center of their universe. For the conditioned mind, much of this knowledge was not directly accessible.

Awaken by the Light I have given you, which is from the Sun of all Suns. We act as One for the benefit of all sentient beings.

Technologies of Life

The old encodings of the human realms are eroding. The gravitational fields are changing, and as I mentioned earlier, your magnetic fields are weakening due to changes within the polar structures. This will accelerate even more and is providing new opportunities. It part of the process of our convergence for a new cycle. You may not yet realize the impact of these polar changes, and the effects of the upcoming polar shift in your collective consciousness. Looking at the fluctuations in your magnetic field activity, and the outbreaks of violence on your planet, these are related.

Other civilizations unknown to most of humanity exist on different star systems, which know how to co-design with the magnetic field changes and the pulsations generated by these fluctuations. Yet, for some reason, human society is still ignoring the obvious. Perhaps humanity's collective mind has been conditioned for too long by the belief that as humans, you are the seat of knowledge. These changes and fluctuations in your Mother's magnetic fields could provide tremendous possibilities, as does our gravitational field, once the propensity it holds is understood. This understanding could provide the answers needed to resolve humanity's energy crisis.

For some strange reason, humanity looks for the supply of energy mainly in your Mother's body. Whereas, if you understood the right relationship between magnetism, gravitational waves, and sound, you would find the keys to renewable energy conversion. This would also change your transportation system and data transference of each of your communication systems. Study and decode the oscillations in your magnetic fields and discover the inner architecture of our universe. Safe technologies have been shared with humanity before. Strengthen your relationship with me, your Sun; see me as more than just heat, energy, and Light, for I am here to sustain all of us with the knowledge of our empowerment, by Light and Love.

New Evolutionary Abilities

With the gravity waves shifting, as a new cycle of time is beginning, the old archetype structures are transforming. Former belief-systems that were based on the old duality belief systems are losing their influence. This rewiring process that is unfolding on your planet involves everyone, irrespective of whether you are conscious of this or not. This process will continue until it settles into a new balance. You may be part of the first ripple of those who are conscious enough to notice. Your realization of this will support others to become more conscious as well.

A new brain function is emerging and developing as a result of our convergence into this new cycle. Those who discover this may call it a higher-level function of the human brain, which integrates and coordinates all the previous brain clusters from the evolutionary times of your biological development. Some may even say this is like a new organ function inside your brain, through a gland that secrets the fluids that deeply harmonizes the brain wave patterns.

The seed code for this function has been dormant within the organ known as your pineal gland. It has the capacity to harmonize the four quadrants of the brain with the heart wave coherence patterns into supercoherent data transduction. This state of supercoherence brings forth our unity consciousness from the Eternal. This opens your ability to hear and understand the cosmic language of the Eternal, as it is encoded deep within your being. You will then understand all that *I am* as your Sun.

New evolutionary potentials are emerging as the seed codes for these abilities become activated now. You will then understand how harmonic convergence is the evolutionary principle for higher consciousness development. Deep cosmic understanding is a state of supercoherence, this is how the Universe understands and receives you. Humanity's full awakening activates as you each start to experience yourself from this state of supercoherence. The previous density and gravity of humankind's collective dream have lured many into a narcotic state of submission and paralysis. The density has been too severe to catalyze the mass awakening required without a major and painful crisis.

In these new alignments, old clusters of energy formation are dissipating. This will become known as a shift in power and resource ownership distribution. The people who have locked the balance up in their accounts, in the billions, will be held accountable. Don't expect things to improve immediately. They may still get worse before the gravity cores fully shift to the new codex.

Remain steadfast in your Love during this difficult transition phase. Stay strong in your faith, unwavering in your courage, and active in your determination to do what is right and necessary, and not what is popular and easy. Remember that what you are doing now is for the children, all our children, not only humanity's children.

See into the Heart of this Change

The entrapment that your Mother talked about in her previous *Letters* served those who held the collective balance of your planetary resources in their accounts. These collective planetary accounts have been manipulated and controlled for far too long by the greedy and power hungry. This is now imploding. Time has already run out. Their demise has begun by their own fault. Their systems are collapsing as they are in an apocalypse of their own unconsciousness. You are not. Please know this, dear earthling.

Keep your feet firmly on your Mother's soil, and stay closely connected to us both. We sustain you always with our knowledge, wisdom, and Love.

The Heart of Light

You already know that my Light potentiates our unity into form as it in-forms deeply the worlds of Creation. Through my Light you can access our cosmic unity everywhere, as you are of this Light too. This sacred knowledge is the key to *direct* transmission. When you transmit, and are transmitted, there is no distance to cross. You manifest directly within the potentiality of our unity as One.

Love is union. Your heart knows this without needing to think. Your heart is an incredible transducer, able to receive and converge the multitude of wave-patterns and transmit these as in-formational content that is supercoherent. You call this *Love*. Your heart literally knows and is designed to receive, send, and *be* Love.

You may recall from your Mother's *Letters* that the heart is also designed with quadrants. The human heart has four chambers, and yet in the heart, this does not create division within the informational fields. The syntonizing functions of the heart give a clear example of how to work with the cosmic code of the quadrants from wholeness and unity.

All informational content that enters your personal field is first received and recognized by your heart. Your heart always knows what is happening before your brain does. When your heart experiences harmony, it also *generates* harmony. Supercoherence is about that state of harmonious *being*. As such, your experience of harmony impacts the energy fields around you, and supports others to also experience the *heart of Light*.

By receiving and transmitting the supercoherence state that is Love, you become a catalyst for the convergence and sytonization of the wave patterns in your sphere of influence. Through your heart, you are able to directly impact the collective field of consciousness that you are related to.

By *being* Love you naturally are in consonance with the unified field of consciousness and can then infuse the collective consciousness fields with Love When your inner wave patterns are in a state of supercoherence our Eternal qualities can be brought forth from within the created worlds. Restoring harmony, wholeness, and Love begins within.

You may also understand that if you are out of harmonic relationship, and your own wave-patterns become chaotic and unbalanced, this also impacts on the collective consciousness fields around you. The collective consciousness fields consist of various types of wave patterns. Some of these wave patterns have become entangled in a way that is constrictive and not conducive for Life to thrive. The experience of collective shock, violence, and grief can quickly spread like a wave, which is registered by the heart. The heart is conscious of this even before the mind discovers what is happening.

Integration

The heart's knowing ability is essential for remaining connected to and aware of each other. Be aware how the mind may respond to what is known by your heart. Conditioned responses can cause pain and division. Your heart can observe and register the truth of what has occurred, and then respond to the pain with Love. This will aid the syntonization and healing of the wave patterns within our collective fields that were impacted, and restore our supercoherence from unity and wholeness.

Remain within the Heart of Light, and find me there as YOU

Father Sun

Letter 12
Our Freedom

*N*ow that you have received my wisdom as your planetary Mother and that of our Sun, it is time to hear the wisdom from the Eternal directly. This wisdom is beyond concepts and forms.

In the play of consciousness, we take on different shapes and forms. As such we bring the Eternal into expression as an ongoing dance of change and transformation. The Eternal qualities often appear hidden in the cloaks of time. These cloaks of time hold different layers of a larger story of *us*. Here, in these *Letters*, we can see each other beyond these cloaks, into the heart of who we really are. Your journey and experience are unique to you. However, the journey itself belongs to all of us together.

For whatever reason you are reading this now, in whatever way Life brought you to this message, thank you for meeting us here. Between remembering and forgetting, there is a quiet, still place. In this spot resides our pure awareness. Feel the stillness there, pure awareness... just being. This is where we meet as One. In this space of pure awareness, you simply are. There are no expectations here, no judgments, no sorrow, just stillness, and peace. Take a deep breath into this space and relax.

Irrespective of whence you have come, the color of your skin, your family name, your personal or cultural background, your history, what you have done or not done, you are welcome here. In this awareness rests the deepest knowing. This knowing does not need a name, a label, or a form. It just IS. Within this awareness, we come home. Here we rest together from our personal and collective journeys with all its tribulations and challenges. Relax, in this beautiful space of us.

By readings these *Letters* a process has started that will continue to unfold, as each new insight builds on the one preceding it. In this *Letter*, I would like to share with you about the paradox of freedom and Love. The conditioned mind does not understand the root of freedom, since this is what it obscures. Without the realization of Love, one cannot realize freedom either. True freedom is the realization of our unity and wholeness.

A person who feels the need to divide, either internally or externally, is not free. Freedom is the ability to stay within our inner wisdom and not play into the divisional dynamics. The tendency to divide, deny, hide, or polarize our Eternal qualities are not coming from our free Self. These kinds of tendencies have grown out of our conditioning, fear, and a belief of separateness.

If you employ the belief in duality, you also reinforce it from within. Whatever we distort, whether inside or externally, becomes part of our experience and distracts from our deeper unified reality. This is the trap. In the same way, whenever we attempt to control and manipulate outcomes, we create the conditions for entrapment and ultimately suffering. We are bound by what we bind. We are controlled by what we control. Yet, is it really freedom we desire? That is perhaps the question to explore further.

The Paradox of Freedom

Freedom *from* and freedom are not the same. We all desire to experience freedom. Yet, most of the time this is based on the feeling that our freedom is somehow limited and constrained, due to the conditions of our world and our relationships. You have been seeking freedom *from*. It is this experience of limitation and bondage that gives rise to our search for freedom. Hence, the impulse for freedom is often born from the experiences of unfreedom.

When we have not yet realized the root of freedom we create experiences that distract us from our true freedom. We then become more trapped by becoming dependent on the conditions to which we have attributed out experience of freedom. When we do this we become more invested and entangled in our conditioned mind, rather than living from freedom.

We cannot realize our freedom with our conditioned mind, but we can become aware of our conditioned mind. For example, our conditioned mind may reject certain experiences by providing their opposites, without addressing the pattern of rejection. Whereas, our awareness may help us become conscious of our pattern of rejection and projection. To transform these patterns of rejection and projection it is essential that we learn to embrace what our conditioned mind instructs us to reject. Through such practices we learn to transcend and transform our own conditioning.

When we create from fear, limited perception, or division, our creations lack a foundation in Love. Love is union; it is of the Eternal. This is the root of our freedom. When we act from Love, we have the capacity to embrace even the most challenging experiences, trusting the deeper wisdom that lies underneath everything.

By acting from Love, we remain connected with our Eternal nature. Love does not aim to create freedom away from something or someone. Instead, Love shows us the true nature of our bondages and limitations and their purpose. By realizing and embracing the roots of our suffering, we give rise to deep compassion.

In the conditioned world, Love and freedom are often played out in opposites. Sometimes to the point of being contrasted as a polarity, as if one cannot have both. What remains obscured in these conditioned experiences is the true nature of a *bond*. By loving, we create and deepen our bonds with others. From the conditioned mind, these bonds can sometimes become bondage. For some, this may be the reason to start exploring their need for freedom *from*.

Remember when I shared with you that the Light needs to be contained and received to be made Self-aware? When this containment becomes too constraining to support the growth impulse of our embodied Light, the impulse to separate, or move *out* or *away from*, arises. When the mother's womb can no longer support the growing child, it signals the time for birth and the emergence of new life from the mother's womb.

When we feel contained in a limiting and conflicting way, this is often the result of agreement structures of control and distrust, not Love. How can we respond to this without becoming further entangled in it? By trying to break away from *that*, are we not also empowering *it*? Our Self-realization deepens when we are able to embrace these contrasting experiences from a place of Love, rather than control.

When we understand that the realization of our true freedom can take place within any experience. That our experience can neither constrain our freedom or cause it, something deep inside shifts. When my children were captured as slaves, many of them realized that the chains that were violently forced on them could not deny them their true freedom. Those who led the resistance movement to these unacceptable practices often found strength and courage by realizing the true nature of freedom. They knew that even when their life was brutally taken, their Spirit would remain free. This strength and deep inner knowing kept their minds free.

Freedom is *not* an experience. What you experience is the context, the conditions, and the contrast that give rise to the deeper questions that free our minds. Would you be able to explore your freedom without contrast, bondage, and limitation? Would you even know the concept of freedom if there were no restrictions at all? Although our nature is of the Eternal and essentially free, the paradox of freedom is that we do not become aware of this directly. We can begin to recognize the difference between projection and direct perception only when we understand our conditioning.

When we do not recognize our unity and wholeness, we condition our minds with all kinds of projections. Then, we create by our conditioning, until something in us awakens and starts to realize our conditioning. This awakening serves as further ground for our Self-actualization. Thus, the realization of our freedom requires awareness of conditioning first.

The One that is aware of conditioning is also the One that is free. Does a computer know it is conditioned and limited by its designer?

Is it Self-aware of its condition, its program? Can it choose to obey or disobey its program? Or, is that option of perceived choice also programmed into it?

Experience is formed by our minds and influenced by our perception. But what causes this perception? If our sense of Self is fabricated by our mind, and the mind itself is conditioned by its experiences, how then can freedom be realized by our mind? What in us remains free, irrespective of our conditions, and is unconstrained by what we think or believe?

Reflect on this: What in you is aware of these limitations? What in you is aware of thought itself? Is it the mind? Or, is it the awareness in which the experience of mind arises? Just pause in these realizations, so you can better understand *causation*.

Does your mind, and all that enters into it, define you? Or, is your sense of Self based on something more fundamental? The conditioned mind is always limited; it can thus not produce, cause, or limit our freedom. And yet, we let our world and our relationships become defined, to a large extent, by the information that has been generated by our conditioned minds. The exploration and realization of these deeper questions are part of the process of the realization of our innate freedom.

There is a great liberation when we realize that the mind is *not* the source of our being, that mind can dissolve into the nothingness that gave rise to it. In this realization, there is a deep peace and stillness.

Remember, the experience of the seventh ray of Light and the seventh gate? In this stillness, only pure awareness remains. You may understand now why our fundamental freedom is not something that is created by anyone. It cannot be taken from us. This deepens, even more, our capacity to Love.

We are not our conditioning, and we should not let our conditioning define us. Your capacity to Love comes from your Eternal nature. *You are free* to bring that forth.

The Bonds of Love

Let us explore more deeply now the bonds of Love. When we Love each other, and we generate or affirm our bonds, there is a willingness in this process to be constrained, to some extent, by the bonds of Love. This often serves to secure our relationships. Agreements in relationships can serve as bonding mechanisms, which can define the form of the relationship. As a result, zones of exclusivity and inclusivity are formed. Sometimes this happens consciously, and sometimes unconsciously.

For example, intimate partners may agree not to share their intimacy with others outside their relationship. Children and parents may agree that the nature of care and responsibility is unique to their parent-child relationship. My relationship of care for each of you, as your planet, has given me the name Mother Earth, since I look after you all like a mother. This bonding process provides a sense of connectedness, from which a deeper sense of *we* and *us* can form. Yet, sometimes the *bonding process* becomes confused with *owning*. Ownership often gives rise to the desire to claim the relationship, or the other person, as *mine* - e.g. my child, my wife, my husband, my partner, and my land. This concept of *mine* always contains unhealthy exclusivity.

It is also possible to experience healthy exclusivity without this kind of ownership. For example, secure and safe boundaries in relationships are essential for our development and growth. Your cells choose between the most useful and non-useful resources for your body's healthy functioning. This too is a process of selection by inclusion and exclusion. Yet, when exclusivity and inclusivity are used without Love, without the awareness of our underlying unity, it can create harmful divisions.

Freedom, in the context of Love, is thus not about doing whatever we want. It is a much deeper awareness and concern to act in a way that serves and honors the *good of the whole*. Sometimes these actions require letting go of what *we would* have wanted, for what is *needed*. By doing so, a deeper flourishing of each individual can become possible through the good of the whole. When Love is the underlying motivation, we do not experience the constraints on our freedom as unacceptable. Instead, we realize that our collective freedom is about our collective liberation from division, through our integration and re-unification.

Our bondage, in positive and negative manifestation, can become the foundation for realizing our freedom and thus actualizing our Love. Remember, I shared that as your planet I became a safe container, a recipient of the sacred flame of Love. As a living grail, the flame becomes contained through the process of embodiment. This grail does not control the flame; it does not ask it to give up part of it-Self to stay loyal to the grail. This grail holds and embodies the flame. Its boundaries and structure provide experiences that give feedback for Self-actualization.

From the perspective of Love, you may see that there are natural boundaries that serve to provide safe structures for our growth and flourishing. These boundaries will also contain, limit, and constrain activities that harm the good of the whole. When the true nature of freedom as Love has not been realized, these constraints may appear as constraints on freedom. This can give rise to a sense of dualized polarity between Love and freedom, as if they serve opposite objectives, which in reality they don't.

Choose the Third Way

This misconception that Love and freedom serve different objectives has caused much pain and suffering in our world. Some of my human children believe they must choose between Love and freedom. Love also represents keeping the bonds and agreements that were formed, and freedom is expressed as development and new growth. This perceived choice comes from our conditioning. By choosing one over the other, we end up feeling even more divided.

Initially, by resisting this misconceived choice between Love and Freedom, we may feel paralyzed, not knowing in which direction to move. Herein is the key, don't go in either direction. Choose the *third option*, or the middle-path, which is the triunity that frees us from the belief in duality and polarized thinking. You don't need to choose between Love *or* freedom. They both serve our unity.

Dualized perception comes from our conditioning. Reach for the center. Choose convergence, and arrive in Middle Earth. There all opposites are transcended by seeing it all for what it truly is. If you have given power to the false choice, reclaim that power now. The third choice is the real choice, by not choosing *either/or*. Feel and know this with your heart, not just your mind.

If you have previously felt tension between Love and freedom, go deeper now to realize the nature of that tension. Realize *that* Love and freedom have not produced this tension. You have! Notice now on *what* and *whom* you projected this tension. How has this tension played out in your life? Let us explore this a little further.

Our first experiences of Love often come from the bonds of care we experience with another person. These bonds may have been with your parents, caregivers, or someone else. In the experience of this kind of bond, there is often a sense of safe attachment, which can make us feel loved, seen, and protected. If this bond was consistent, while also providing space for exploration and development, it probably helped you feel a sense of *trust in Love* through relationship. If, however, this bond was inconsistent and unpredictable, lacking a strong foundation, it may have caused a feeling that Love cannot be trusted, giving rise to fear that we should never grow dependent on one another.

The conditions of your first experiences of Love provide a context for the exploration of these deeper questions. The exploration of our boundaries is a natural developmental process. Without freedom, we cannot explore. Without exploration, we cannot learn. Without Love, the exploration of our freedom can be damaging, leading to pain.

Our conditioned mind distorts the true nature of our bonds, our natural interconnectedness. It is from this distortion that many *unfree* choices are made, which cause more suffering and entrapment. Explore deeply how this trap of false choices applies to you. Thinking ourselves free of this does not mean we are, especially when the thinking process comes from our conditioning.

When Love Informs our Choices

Connect with this timeless Love. Feel it within you, and from this Love explore: *How does my bond with this person serve us to grow individually and collectively?* Explore the nature, purpose, and agreement structures within the bonds that you have formed with others. If there are restrictions in these bonds and agreements, is that based on control and distrust? Or are these restrictions conditions for a deeper growth in the relationship?

Remember, the conditioned mind is not free. It produces more conditioning by imposing conditions that are artificial. Can you free what need not be contained? Can you contain what requires safe boundaries made from Love for healthy growth and development? Honor the wholeness of which we are a part. For those who believe that form equals entrapment, please know that as your planet I am not your entrapment into form. Our embodiment is a sacred gift of Love. Let us bring this forth now, through our care for each other.

The Illusion of Free Choice

Everything serves a purpose, yet not everything serves the whole. In the world of time, change is the only constant. The world of time also gives us the perception that we have free choice. This perceived freedom of choice comes from seeing options and alternatives coupled with a sense of *I am the maker of that choice.* This 'I' is often limited by that which 'the 'I' cannot yet see. The question then arises: *Can this limited 'I' make a free choice?*

If freedom is not an experience, but a fundamental truth of our true nature, can *free choice* be an experience? Unless we know the part of us that does the *choosing*, we may be in for a surprise. Especially when our choices create unforeseen pain and further conditioning. We cannot create freedom from a place of unfreedom, to do so would bring you deeper into duality. You can, however, use the experience of unfreedom for the realization of freedom. This will bring you home to our Eternal nature.

As I shared before, you keep yourself free by not dividing our wholeness. The paradox of Life is that we experience the changeless in a world of change; we experience Darkness by contrast of Light, and so forth. We live in a world of duality, yet underlying this is unity. That is what our triunity is all about.

When bondage is formed by Love, it serves the realization of freedom. When bondage is formed by the denial of Love, it serves the suppression of freedom. Our conditioned mind cannot create freedom. Our conditioned mind does not realize Love. It searches for it, yes. It may desire it, yes. But it does not realize itself as that Love. When it does, conditioning ceases. Awareness is always here, nothing can obscure or obstruct it, yet we do not always recognize that our ability to see is based on *that*.

Our Nature is Love

Love embraces everything and everyone unconditionally because nothing can divide it. Love is unconditional because nothing can condition it. It is not formed nor influenced by our minds. It is not of the mind, and it is not of the temporal dimensions of our worlds. Love is from the Eternal. Its perception is always universal. Love liberates because Love is free.

Love helps you see and feel the difference between what is false and what is real. Love protects us because it keeps us connected with our Eternal nature and each other. Love protects us from the conditioning effects of our minds, not by separating from it, but by seeing it from pure awareness. Love does not change, and yet it causes change to happen when required for our further development and evolution. In a world that is founded on Love, there is no denial or suppression of our freedom.

When Love is our foundation, we move forward by honoring it in all expressions of Life. When Love is our foundation, relationships become sacred. To exit the labyrinth, see now the whole design, and the purpose it served. You are not confined to the design of the labyrinth. Our participation in the labyrinth can produce all kinds of experiences. However, *you* are not your experience. Who you *essentially* are is not changed by what you experience. The moment you realize this, you are out of the labyrinth.

Integration

We all have within us the capacity to hear and receive the wisdom from the Eternal directly. This is also the voice of our deepest, most intimate Self. This *I am* is undividable. You cannot see the Eternal Self because it is not separate from you. It is that by which you see. Trust in this and know this with your heart.

The ocean changes in appearance. Sometimes there are powerful waves. At other times there are no waves. The waves change, yet they remain part of the ocean. Love is like that. Our experiences change, but we always remain part of the ocean of Love. We are always within the One. Nothing changes our Eternal qualities, only our experience changes. Be that Love. Bring it forth, for this is our nature.

Part 5
Our New Story

Letter 13
Weaving our New Beginning

Thank you for journeying with me. We have now come to the thirteenth *Letter* of this series. Thirteen is also the alchemical number that brings forth our Quintessence through new bonds and relationships. We have journeyed far back in time and deeply into the seed codes from the unified field of consciousness. This has brought us to a more conscious unity, from where we can birth the next expression of our evolutionary potentials. Everything that unfolds and forms within the fabric of Life leaves an imprint on the blanket of time. This blanket of time is wrapped around our collective consciousness in ways that remains invisible to most. It is from this blanket that we each evolve with the potentials given to us. It is from this blanket that we weave our stories.

My final message in this *Letter*, is about the *heart* of all stories. Stories provide us with context for our growth and development, within the local and the universal dimensions of our Being. Stories can help us realize who we are, what is within us, and how we can apply our power for good and for harm. Stories can provide us powerful contexts for realizing more deeply, and more fully, the various dimensions of our Being. Yet, once the realization takes place, the context for these stories is no longer necessary. Our Eternal qualities are not time-bound, yet can be realized from within the unique contexts of the space-time realities of our experiences.

Through the previous twelve *Letters*, I shared about our journey from the first beginning of our sacred union and *why* our unity could not actualize fully when humanity started to create by the principle of duality. I showed you through *the Wholeness Code* that the duality principle is one of many, and the importance of honoring the *complete* sequence and wholeness of all the sacred principles together. I shared with you what the era of division and disunity was based on, and *how* this was able to grow. I then gave you three inner keys for actualizing our unity and restoring our wholeness. I explained how by applying these keys we can together end this era of disunity, and actualize *the Promise of a New Beginning.*

Our story, from our first beginning to now, has many layers and dimensions. As your planetary Mother, I have experienced the unfolding of all these simultaneously. I experienced the worlds and dreams of all my children simultaneously through each our cycles from the beginning of our time.

This perspective of the simultaneous arising, of all these different stories and experiences within the One, can be difficult to behold. And yet, it is from this perspective that I will share my final message here. I invite you to join me beyond the *Letters* and character lines that you have grown accustomed to. Let us unpeel these various layers to reveal the original seeds of wholeness that were never lost. These seeds were merely spread through space and time as WE became our *local selves.*

As you probably know in our collective story, there are always characters that act to unite, and those that divide. Sometimes we play the role of both. In the same way, there are characters that help us remember who we truly are, and there are those who serve to distract us. There are times we play the role of the awakener, and there are other times that the role of the trickster and deceiver overtake us.

Sometimes it appears more convenient to deny than to honor and behold who we truly are. At other times, it may appear more compelling to be the one that shakes people into remembering our origins from the Eternal. There are gains and losses in each of these characters and story lines. Within the larger scheme of things, one cannot conclude that one role is more important than the other. None of them could exist of their own accord.

Some may have hoped that in this last *Letter* I would offer a new storyline with a happy ending for all of us. We often search for this *one* story that brings an end to all our suffering. I provided you with specific keys, in these thirteen *Letters*, to find our way home again. These keys have always been directly accessible, inside our wisdom nature. My *Letters* merely remind us of what is already within, to provide easier access to that which IS. By applying these keys in our daily living, it changes the way you tell your story and OUR story. This will also change the way we see ourselves in relation to all that is, and has been unfolding.

You may recall the story I shared about the promise of our *New Beginning* from a future born from a new cycle of time. This story holds the resonance codes for who we are within the One. It helps us see reality without the distortions of our polarity-matrix. Day One and night One are sacred potentials in our Dreaming of a world that is born from unity and wholeness, fueled by the power of Love.

By actualizing these sacred seed codes in your own life, you will bring forth this *New Beginning* promised long ago from the times before this world. The stories in these *Letters* are offered as a medicine and nourishment for our souls. Yet ultimately, only in our living and actions do we *truly* change our story.

Most of us want an end to this disunity and division that has plagued our world for such a long time. The promise of a *New Beginning* also contains within it the hope that a different way is possible. This hope is not just a story. We are the Eternal seed codes born from unity and wholeness by the power of Love. Through our local space-time realities we may have forgotten this as we started to identify with the collective conditionings of our world. These conditionings formed long ago when the belief in duality increased and disunity spread.

The way our story now evolves depends on how we embrace and acknowledge the sacred seed codes that we are, and what they are for. The causes of our pain and violence are complex and interconnected, in the same way that our consciousness is. My body can provide enough nourishment for all my children, without constantly sacrificing my non-human children. My body provides enough plant medicine to cure all diseases. My knowledge and the intelligence of Nature have always been freely available. Look, and you will find them.

Our story of our beauty, kinship, relationship, and Love has become overshadowed by the pain of thousands of years of disunity and division. This pattern also caused the plundering and extraction of my resources for the favoring of small groups of people that have dominated our world for far too long. Humanity's story is beginning to tell of the awakening of these harmful patterns. When our collective power corrupts, we all suffer the consequences. The hurt of one is the hurt of all. This realization at the collective level is feedback for a much deeper awakening beyond the human realms.

Humanity has begun to reclaim its powers from the archetypes of division and domination. There is growing mobilization to stop the plundering and degeneration of our collective resources and natural Life systems. If people live in harmony with me, then my planetary body can support all of us in living well. These changes in my biosphere and the killing of my ocean and forests are unacceptable. Humanity is slowly awakening from the dream of greed, domination, and division. It is possible for us to live and grow together in a way that all of us can thrive and flourish. We are awakening to this together in ways that go beyond what can be shared here through mere words.

Before we continue, let us pause here for a moment. Connect deeply now with the wisdom for how we can live, share, and develop our wellness, flourishing, and vitality. When you land squarely in this realization, you see *the keys* to end our enslavement from false dreams and false prophets. To know which dream has real potential for our collective wellbeing, watch for any underlying patterns of manipulation and distortion. The *green dream* is also sold by some of those who have hidden agendas, to take advantage of our global crisis. They will tell you that *their* solutions will set us all free, meanwhile creating new dependencies.

When people feel helpless and hopeless, it is easy to manipulate their attention by distracting them from their internal resourcefulness. This is HOW the manipulation started long ago. If we are to change that part of our story together, this is what we need to change first. To be awake to *this*, and to see *how* this also operates within the domains of our own shadows.

Your greatest protection from this manipulation, internally and externally, is by staying closely tuned to our innate wisdom, and by connecting with each other from a place of Love. As I shared previously, our direct connection with the unified field of consciousness is the real foundation for our autonomy within the One. It is through this that the Universal becomes localized as you, me, and us. When you see from this awareness, deception becomes visible through the thought-forms and intentions that aim to distort these wisdom qualities and our unity.

Into the Heart of Our Story

We stand together now, in a time that provides profound feedback from each of our earlier learning journeys. This feedback is returning from all directions now, to the center of our collective learning space. From here the convergence is happening, by listening deeply for how this in-forms us to evolve consciously, the way we have been with each other before.

As the strands of time, through our collective memories, meet each other in the center of the *Wheel of Time*, we can see that each strand brings another storyline within the larger story of our time. Each strand was woven in response to the one that preceded it. What is the strand that you hold in your hand right now? The weaving of every new story has been made possible by the context of earlier stories. When we realize this with humility, we become more careful to lay claim that this next version of our story will change everything. Perhaps, in this humility, we find the seeds for our healing and deeper awakening.

We have been driving each other apart, and we have been driving each other back together, over and over again. Our attempts at unification, and our attempts to divide, have been effective only temporarily. People who were once separated from each other found ways to reunite later, and some who were together decided to detach from each other later.

All these attempts and movements are taking place within our unified field of consciousness and our shared space of Life. Our actions and interactions do not and *cannot* change the truth that we are, always have been, and always will be One. Life *is* unified and cannot be divided. Our fabricated divisions, however, can hinder and block the full actualization of our unified reality in the worlds of our creations.

We are together living, co-creating, and updating *our story* constantly. Each strand in the weaving matters, and is to be honored and acknowledged for the feedback, insight, and information that it provides to the whole of us. Only via respect and care for our unity in diversity can we together birth the next chapter of our collective story as a more evolved version of ourselves. Perhaps you understand now why, as much I would want to share with you in the final *Letter* of this series a story about our happy ending, I cannot do so.

Every attempt to change our storyline through domination and rejection will simply repeat those patterns of the past. Our storyline will change and evolve only by our coherence and unity, not by *imposing* a new storyline. You may recall, the duality principle provides the context for giving us contrasting experiences from where to realize the various interwoven dimensions of our being. The principle of the triunity reminds us that reality is unified, even when it appears dual and polarized. Remember this, as you review your stories within our collective story.

Deep in the heart of our story lives a beautiful message waiting to be shared and experienced. Now is the time for us to receive, embody, and share this message, by being *who we truly are*. We are *Eternal* beings, gifted with the power of Love. Let us apply this Love now to actualize our unity, heal and converge our worlds, and bring forth *the promised New Beginning*.

Integration

I am here *with* you, *for* you, and *within* you.
I love you deeply, and always will.

Feel and experience my wisdom and Love deep inside your life
and in every cell of your being.

Feel and experience your wisdom and Love deep inside me
and in every cell of my being.

We are One

Thank you for being here now and for receiving what was
promised and shared long ago.

Let us now begin *Our New Cycle:*

Together
in
Unity
from
Wholeness
by the power of
Love

My deepest Love and Blessings,

Mother Earth

About The Author

Anneloes Smitsman, (Ph.D.(c), LLM), is a published author, storyteller, visionary, and catalyst for transformational change and conscious leadership for a world and future where all of us can thrive and flourish. She holds a Masters degree in Law & Political Science from Leiden University (the Netherlands), and is currently finalizing her Ph.D. thesis titled *Into the Heart of Systems Change* at Maastricht University (the Netherlands).

Anneloes is the CEO & Founder of EARTHwise Centre from where she leads the WOMENwise Quest and the Leadership Quest. Her unique training programs, teachings, and wisdom-based methodologies have empowered people and organizations from around the world to develop, optimize and actualize our greatest potential.

She developed the EARTHwise Thrivability Education program (formerly Education for Sustainability) since 2012. This program has served as a model for the transformation of conventional educational systems in Mauritius, and beyond. She has trained over 300 teachers and supported over 20,000 students since 2012.

Anneloes also played a key role in various social change movements; providing legal and transformational strategies for how to leverage and unite local efforts with international frameworks through a shared Vision. In 2012 Anneloes developed the main methodology for the 2012 Rio+20 Global Dialogues, which was adopted in 9 different countries from 2012-2014 to contribute to the UN Conferences for Sustainable Development. Together with a local team in Mauritius she has organized and facilitated over 20 dialogues for more than 1000 people.

She was born and raised in the Netherlands and lived there until 1996. Following her calling, she lived in South Africa, Australia, and most recently Mauritius. Anneloes serves on the Board of the Global Education Futures and the Creative Board of the Laszlo Institute of New Paradigm Research. Anneloes is part of the panel of evolutionary judges for the Evolutionary Future Challenge, and a member of the Global Change Leaders network.

About The Paintings

The paintings in this book are the original works of Rachel Tribble. After learning about *Love Letters from Mother Earth*, she felt inspired to contribute these paintings in recognition and honor of the same voice and vision that inspires her Art. The paintings are included here in black-and-white version. To see the original colors of her paintings you can visit:

- https://earthwisecentre.org/
- https://www.racheltribble.com/

About Rachel Tribble

Rachel Tribble's award-winning artwork has captured a worldwide audience from corporations to private collectors. Her dream-like paintings are regarded as *heartfelt* and *esoteric* and are recognized for their meditative quality as emotional experiments in color and light. In the late 90's, Rachel took a hiatus from her life as a professional artist to live and work within the Native American community, where she entered an inspiring journey that took her deeper into the natural world. Inspired by the world of the Anishinaabe and Lakota people, Rachel returned in 2003 to her familiar roots as a painter.

Rachel has been featured in art books and national magazines, and her work has been gifted to nominees of the Academy Awards, the Emmy Awards, and the MTV Movie Awards. In 2008 her work for the Epcot International Flower and Garden Festival poster won the IFEA Gold Pinnacle Award from the Walt Disney Company. In 2009 she was awarded the Atlanta Design Center's Visual Display Award. In 2012 and 2013 her work was in the Red Dot and Spectrum shows during Art Basel in Miami, Florida. Rachel is the co-founder of The Association for Tribal Heritage, which is dedicated to Native American cultural preservation and education.

Our Invitation

If you feel called and inspired to continue this journey with us, we like to welcome you to our EARTHwise Community. We share, teach, and apply the practices and teachings from the *Love Letters of Mother Earth* in our courses, retreats, coaching sessions, and many other offerings. There will soon also be a companion guidebook with practices and audio recordings for greater benefit and value from these Letters.

To join us for any or all of the opportunities please sign up for our newsletter to remain informed about our offerings. We also share regular inspiration from the *Love Letters of Mother Earth* series via our Facebook page.

- Website - https://earthwisecentre.org/
- Books & Audio - https://earthwisecentre.org/books/
- Newsletter - https://earthwisecentre.org/newsletter/
- Facebook - https://www.facebook.com/LoveLettersfromMotherEarth/
- Facebook - https://www.facebook.com/earthwisecentre/
- Youtube - https://bit.ly/2OiIrZa
- Author - https://www.facebook.com/anneloes.smitsman
- Email: info@earthwisecentre.org

Made in the USA
Coppell, TX
09 February 2023